THE DIRT[illegible]

Alister Esam was a frustrated CEO an[illegible]
about his business he was working 80 hours a week trying to make everything perfect. At the same time he drove his employees up the wall. Disempowering them to the point that they could no longer contribute to the business, demotivating them and heaping more stress on himself.

He found salvation in a surprising place. People associate process with control, monotony, routine, the status quo and with an overall death of creativity. It's a Dirty Word they try to avoid.

Alister discovered that if implemented correctly it provided empowerment, autonomy and creativity for employees and delivered business freedom for himself with total reassurance his business was running itself.

It also enabled him to massively accelerate improvement in his business by harnessing his team's collective brainpower.

This book looks at why process is so important, why people get it so wrong and make it so horrible and how to put it in place in a new way which can change the whole culture of a business.

THE DIRTY WORD

The dirty word that is surprisingly the key to business freedom

ALISTER ESAM

COPYRIGHT

Published by Alister Esam.

Printed by Book Printing UK www.bookprintinguk.com

Remus House, Coltsfoot Drive, Peterborough, PE2 9BF

Printed in Great Britain.

ISBN 978-1-9196131-0-9

For Victoria

CONTENTS

1

FIRST THINGS FIRST

"The Dirty Word"

My wife doesn't really know what I do for a living. I mean, she has a rough idea - but what I do doesn't interest her. We have an old-fashioned relationship by mutual consent. I earn the money; she looks after the children and the house. She doesn't care much about my work as long as I'm happy.

As a result, my wife's friends really don't have a clue what I do other than that I run a business called Process Bliss.

One of these friends came for lunch recently. As it happens, I used to work with her husband. She's a friend of mine too: I've known her personally for 30 years.

The interaction I describe here is a typical one.

I wander downstairs from my office around lunchtime and this friend and my wife are chatting at the kitchen island. The friend looks up, notices me and says: "Here he comes, Mr Process."

The conversation continues; I smile silently. The friend expands on her description, joking about how organised I am - inferring that I am boring and unspontaneous.

My wife joins in the teasing, echoing and agreeing with these sentiments. The woman I have been with since the age of 17 is teasing me for being the complete opposite of what I am.

Now the truth is that, in my head, chaos reigns. I cannot remember to do anything. I struggle to concentrate on things for more than a few seconds before becoming distracted. Left to my own devices, I am easily bored – to the point that I will do straightforward tasks differently every time. Whenever I travel somewhere, I will return a different way so that I get to see twice as much.

At work I drive people up the wall because I'm always changing things, looking for better ways to do them; forgetting why we go about things a certain way in the first place. I suggest things I know will never work just to see where it takes the conversation.

I'm spontaneous: I'll suggest a family holiday 24 hours before we are due to go. I have the sort of brain that, when someone suggests we do something, will struggle to resist the temptation to make it happen right there and then.

I despise rules and when I come across them, I feel instinctively that I want to break them - just for the sake of it. Like when we went to see the golden Buddha in Bangkok and were told by the tour guide that it was very bad luck to cross a certain threshold to a doorway. As soon as no one was looking - it seemed offensive to do it in front of her - I felt compelled to cross it.[1]

I fly planes and helicopters, sail boats, race cars, do parachute jumps and I take pride in deliberately walking or jogging through the more dubious parts of dangerous cities – going on to tell the locals where I've been (to gauge their reaction and establish just how dangerous my choice really was). One time with my 12-year-old daughter, on seeing a volcano erupting in the distance, we immediately dropped our plans to visit Ikea and headed towards the plume of ash, before proceeding to climb to the top to get a closer view.

Yet, here I am, sitting in my kitchen hearing myself described as Mr Boring, Mr Predictable, Mr Routine.

All because of this one dirty word: Process.

The truth is, I need tools to keep order in my life; to help manage the chaos that would otherwise ensue - and process has been the most powerful of these aids. But I have had to make it work for my chaotic persona, because that is one variable that is not going to change.

And yes, as a result, I am amazingly organised. In many respects I run my life like a well-oiled machine. But that's because I have developed tools and techniques to enable that.

---

[1] To be fair my daughter actually beat me to this so it may be a family trait.

Just as a blind person might develop better hearing to compensate for the ability they are missing, I have created these utilities to fill in for my serious organisational inadequacies. And clearly they are very effective – because people now assume those organisational qualities to be integral to who I am.

My aim, in this short preface, is to address and move on from this idea that 'process' is a dirty word; something to recoil from. As my personal example highlights, the connotations of this word can be incredibly negative.

The notion of 'process' fills people with dread: it feels like something onerous - to be avoided. You may have considered abandoning this book as soon as you discovered what the Dirty Word was. Thank you for carrying on.

Yet process shouldn't be off-putting. For me personally, it allows me to achieve everything I want whilst retaining all the best qualities of my chaotic self.

And it has become the same for me in business.

When I found myself as an accidental CEO of my own company (I never set out to be a CEO; I suspect few CEOs do), I had built a business which was more chaotic even than my personal life – something that made me, and consequently my staff, miserable.

I needed to find a way to retain the creativity, innovation and energy, but manage it in a non-chaotic way. Process, that dirty word in business, enabled me to do this - but not in the way most people would imagine; not in a rigid, rule-enforcing manner.

My hope is that this book will change your perception of process and allow it to help you get your business in order - without killing the creativity or the fun, or subjecting your people to all the other negative misconceptions that go with it.

2

INTRODUCTION

"Leaders don't force people to follow—they invite them on a journey" - Charles S. Lauer[2]

Imagine if success - or successful practice - was something you could bottle. If you could capture all the things that make a company great, different, special and turn them into something repeatable – and *reliably* and *consistently* so. Ultimately this is what business is about: creating and perfecting a product and surrounding experience, and then doing more of the same.

This is the essence of **process** – which the Collins dictionary defines as 'a method of operation'; and/or 'a series of actions or changes'. Or, as a verb, process is 'handling, treating or preparing by special method (of manufacture, etc)'.

It is all of these elements combined which, to me, separate one company from another. In other words, it is in the detail of *process* that an organisation's special ingredients lie. And it is through the pursuit, capture, packaging and execution of good process that a business owner/manager can expect to achieve a state of fulfilment, even bliss - as

[2] Charles S. Lauer, US magazine publisher, columnist, public speaker and author of *Soar with the eagles*; and *Reach for the stars: Pursuing success through excellence.*

the organisation begins to deliver the expected results - without compromising their own health or happiness.

So why is it that so many businesses leave process to chance and others treat it with disdain, like some sort of dirty word?

...X...

Paul, public relations consultant to my company Process Bliss, used to work at a large PR firm with about 20 people. He recalls that the company once had some really nice touches as part of its process for welcoming new customers on board. For example, newly signed-up clients would receive a nice glossy sheet with photos of the team, along with their contact details, Twitter handles and other useful details. This simple gesture made new customers feel valued and an extension of the team. Yet one day, for no particular reason, this activity stopped.

Sadly, this inconsistency in experience is all too common in the workplace. Teams have wonderful, creative ideas which are agreed and built into the way the business operates, with intentions of an enduring, positive impact. But, for reasons that are difficult to fathom, these extra flourishes or value-added activities peter out, are distorted, or just cease without warning.

Inevitably, the associated benefits dry up too, and managers and employees become frustrated at the organisation's inability to make its good intentions stick. Over time, people across the business lose faith in the company's commitment to innovation, and become demotivated.

They stop coming up with creative ideas, knowing that while process embellishments might be honoured for a while, behaviour will revert to default settings within a few months, so what's the point?

When a manager tries to challenge this inertia, the risk is that they will find themselves working 18 hours a day - as I did - to police quality and perfection in the business. As well as being unsustainable for the manager, this typically demotivates employees further still; now they feel they are being controlled and hounded – not trusted to do a good job without systematic oversight.

If, as a business leader, you have experienced these kinds of challenges and are at a loss about how to make positive changes stick in your business; if you're frustrated that your business is not running as well as it could be – or, if you work for a company and are ambitious in your ideas for improving existing processes, this book is for you.

From one process innovator to another

Perhaps you're like me – you started your business brimming with enthusiasm for what you would achieve, only to find yourself working lots of late nights with that anticipated sense of accomplishment never quite drawing any nearer. Over time, you've come to feel as though you're the only one who cares enough about the business to want to make a difference.

When I told a CEO friend of mine that I had sold my old business and then started a new one, after her initial congratulations she expressed her horror at my decision to get back in the "driving seat". She had been running her business for 5 years and these were her exact words: *"I Reckon when this chapter of my life finishes I want to find a hut in a field overlooking some sea and never touch anything to do with business ever again. In summary, it is so, so, so hard and I'm pretty tired. My mojo is getting pretty worn down. Living the start up "dream"."*

I used to feel like this. But I found a way out. In this book I will chart my journey from feeling encumbered, exhausted, never satisfied with my business, to feeling confident I could distance myself from its everyday operation, without risk of calamity or chaos. I'll share insight into how I empowered my employees to drive processes themselves and, ultimately, run and shape the business, allowing me to release my tight grip on the reins.

The key was discovering the enabling potential of 'process'. This might sound like a contradiction in terms – the word 'process' is generally associated with something uninspiring, 'corporate', controlling and unpleasant - a "dirty word" which whenever muttered invokes thoughts of a dreaded stifling bureaucracy; a "dirty word" which encapsulates all the worst aspects of work.

However, I was able to reframe process as a positive business tool, which was truly liberating for me, and empowering for the people I worked with.

Strong, effective process is something that will enable your business to run like a well-oiled machine, while simultaneously releasing you so that you are no longer bound to it day and night. I went from working an 80-

hour week as a hands-on, meddling business manager to putting in just 14 hours a week as a strategic business leader. (There is a big difference between these two interpretations of the remit of an MD or CEO, which I'll discuss later in this book.)

I believe you could transform your own role in much the same way, and will show you how.

When I eventually sold my previous business in 2018, it was in fantastic shape. What's more, I was able to extract myself within just two weeks. By then my team were pretty much running the business and didn't really need me. And that's all because I had put the right processes in place. What's more, I was able to *prove* to the business purchasers that due process was being followed. And that employees embraced, and took ownership of, everything that went on.

Today I see many other business owners in the same relentlessly stressed-out state I was in before I saw the light and set myself free - and I *know* that I can help them. I founded my current company, Process Bliss, to do exactly that – by providing simple process software, accessible online, that anyone can apply and use to transform the way they operate.

Why make running a business harder than it needs to be?

It's extremely common, that sense of wanting the company you created to be perfect and of feeling the need to stay on top of that. Although the people who work for you may be good, and keen to drive improvements, inevitably they won't be as invested as you are as the business creator and owner.

As the ultimate driver of high standards, inevitably you're drawn into correcting and spotting little things day to day. You probably set reminders to check up on the jobs you want to be done, the loose ends you want to tie up before you can relax and move on.

As your business gets bigger, this constant vigilance becomes overwhelming. You either work yourself to the bone (without ever managing to keep on top of things), or are forced to lower your expectations and standards, accepting that few things in this life are perfect, people have flaws, and the only way to preserve your sanity is to accept the way things are.

These are both depressing scenarios, and it can be hard to see another path. This is where I believe I can help.

How this book can help you

I hope this book will serve as a roadmap to process-enabled freedom.

I'll begin by encouraging you to reflect on what makes your business special, and consider why process matters – that is, the role it will or should play in maintaining that market edge, so that your business continues to succeed.

I'll explore why process gets such a bad press, why employees often rebel against it, and how process can go wrong for companies.

Having identified what 'bad' looks like, I'll examine how to flip that picture and make process a *positive* business *enabler* - for employees, for customers, ***and*** for business owners - so that their collective fire continues to burn brightly.

I'll look at process from a number of different angles, highlighting how prevalent it is across business and in our lives, and illustrate the power of great process in a range of scenarios. Finally, I'll offer some practical suggestions about how you might build effective process into your own organisation and its everyday practices.

By the end of the book, I hope you will be inspired to embrace process with new determination, as a means to rediscovering your passion for business – or, if you're a driven employee, your role within it. Alternatively, if your goal is to move on from your current company, I hope this book will equip you with the right tools so that you can start to release control, knowing your business will soon be running itself.

3

WHAT MAKES YOUR BUSINESS SPECIAL?

When did you last reflect on your company's unique selling proposition: its differentiating features that keep customers coming back? These may seem obvious, but it's possible that somewhere along the line priorities have changed, or conflicted, and some of that differentiation has been eroded over time. Or perhaps the business as a whole is not geared to supporting and reflecting the same outcomes - or not in a deliberate, consistent and repeatable way.

A business's value proposition can take many forms. It could be linked to physical assets (*eg* property, or a fleet of vehicles); a network of skilled people; or some kind of stronghold on a market.

For most businesses, however, differentiation is strongly linked to its ethos and brand experience. If a customer can find equivalent products or services at a similar or better price point from other sources, their likelihood of choosing one company over another will be dictated by their perception of how well their needs will be met, how convenient the experience is, how helpful the staff are, and so on.

Managing customer expectations

Research abounds about the importance of the customer experience in determining brand loyalty. Customers who had a very good experience are three and a half times more likely to buy again from a business, and five times more likely to recommend it to others, than following a poor experience, according to research by Temkin[3].

I can vouch for this personally. Many years ago, my family and I stumbled across a wonderful hotel in the New Forest in the UK, which served as a place of blissful refuge during a particularly testing camping trip. Our experience of the hotel and its employees left such a positive imprint on us that we returned to stay there many times over the years to come. From the handwritten notes welcoming us back each time, to the fact that the staff remembered our names, we felt valued and looked after. Nothing was too much trouble. When we discovered the same company also had hotels in other parts of the UK, we sought them out and continued to enjoy the same positive experience.

Over a period of about 15 years, we spent tens of thousands of pounds with this hotel chain. That was until the time we were made to feel that our loyal custom counted for nothing – when we were forced to cancel a booking within 71 hours, marginally contravening the terms of their refund policy by 1 hour.

I'll come back to this experience in a later chapter, but suffice to say that the way the company handled our case - particularly in the light of all of our years of loyalty and custom - was sufficiently disappointing to undermine everything that had gone before. Next time we decided to stay with a competitor which we also loved. The magic spell was broken and

[3] Customer Experience Matters, Temkin 2018.

our loyalty turned out to be very fragile. It is rare that we return to their hotels now.

Earning a positive brand reputation is hard work; losing it is worryingly easy.

Brand tools including logos, colour schemes and so on may provide clues to a business's proclaimed values, but if those values are not reflected reliably across every experience everywhere they will soon attract negative associations.

One of my family's favourite places to eat is Wagamama. We love the food and, no matter which branch we visit, we know exactly what we're going to get. This isn't a restaurant in which you can while away an afternoon, the experience is quick and efficient. If we want a meal in 40 minutes - for example when we're on the road or have a little time before our film starts at the cinema – Wagamama is the perfect choice.

The chain's success is down to its formula – it's consistent, repeatable process and the reliable experience this creates. Wherever you may be in the world, eating at Wagamama feels familiar and reassuring. Expectations have been set, and are consistently met.

The whole experience in these restaurants has been designed to be efficient. For instance, meals are designed to be cooked quickly, and it's always made clear that dishes will be served as they come (rather than when everything is ready). Staff don't waste time on pleasantries, either. When - often rather abruptly they ask a customer if they are happy with their meal, they'll scribble a note on the individual's tablemat to confirm that this exchange has taken place – this simple and quite crude measure ensures that everyone is asked, but never more than once.

The process is designed to ensure people have an enjoyable meal but vacate their table relatively quickly, therefore maximising the number of covers they can serve in any given day. Eating at Wagamama may feel like a production line rather than a fine-dining experience, but it is what it is, and the model is ideal for the purpose of creating happy customers and maximising profit.

Formalising finesse

It may seem strange to think of process as a differentiator, given its link to intended consistency: it could easily be seen as a negative force, imposed by managers to kill creativity and personal initiative. But it's actually the opposite.

Take real estate agencies. On the face of it, these companies all look the same. They charge approximately the same fee and all do a very similar thing. If I'm selling my house, they will list my property with an online aggregator (such as Rightmove in the UK), promote it, liaise with potential buyers, and show them the property if I require them to. As a vendor, other than being assured of a good result, I don't really care which brand of agent I go to.

But when you step inside their offices, you start to see what differentiates one brand from another: how attentive and professional the staff are; how inviting the environment might seem to a purchaser wishing to browse or view properties; whether staff seem trustworthy, on top of their game, approachable and keen to understand a client's particular needs.

If there is no specified process, and the experience being delivered has been left up to individual account handlers and their own personal style, there may be immediate discrepancies between one client's experience and the next.

Process and associated staff training, on the other hand, will ensure that every time someone walks through the door, they have a consistent experience – that which the business owner or senior management team has defined as reflecting the company's brand values.

Establishing a baseline experience you can build on

Setting down agreed parameters makes life easier for everyone – for employees who now have a clear guide to what's expected of them and how to do it; and for process owners who can start to ease off on the controls, knowing that business is being done the way they need it to be done.

Once the essence of the experience you want to create has been rolled out through agreed process, you can look to *improve* that experience based on feedback from employees and clients, and other insights from the wider market. By now, you're providing something better than your competitors. When someone walks into one of your agency locations, they receive a consistent, predictable service aligned to the overall brand of the business. They can rely on that experience, and they can confidently recommend the service experience to others, knowing that they too will encounter the same value.

Consistent process shouldn't simply apply to creating the right environment, but rather it should extend to all aspects of what you do. Staying with the house-selling/house-purchasing scenario, this includes the steps that are taken across the engagement.

Take house viewings, for example. You may want to ensure that when someone looks around a property on your books it will smell of baked bread and coffee, and have a vase of freshly cut flowers in the kitchen. These small value-added details can subtly influence prospective purchasers, while demonstrating initiative to the property vendor.

Mapping out desirable behaviour in a repeatable process distinguishes a superior service from a run-of-the-mill agency.

Inviting everyone on the journey

The same principles can be applied to any business, in any market. Any organisation that wants to be different from its competitors needs to create a template for best practice, and document it for others to follow.

The key to making this a positive development for all is something we will explore in more detail later. This is about making sure employees can see the benefit in the proposed process, and are given a chance to contribute to it with their own suggestions and feedback. Once they can see how the documented process will make their own lives easier, the chances are they will willingly embrace it and make it their own.

This is critical to the lasting success of process. Once everyone buys into it and can see the benefits, process begins to gain a momentum of its own, as teams and individuals spot additional tweaks that could raise the game again.

This is important because, if your process generates visible success, the chances are that your rivals will notice and emulate your approach, potentially adding an even better twist. To maintain the lead you have created, you'll need to continuously evolve and improve what you're doing.

In summary, to run a business with clearly differentiated value you will need to have control over how your business operates, and a mechanism for managing and improving process.

"If your process generates visible success, the chances are that your rivals will notice and emulate your approach, potentially adding an even better twist. To maintain the lead you have created, you'll need to continuously evolve and improve what you're doing."

4

WHY PROCESS MATTERS

Process exists in every business; otherwise how would it operate? But if everyone is following their own process, or bending the rules to fit the way they prefer to work, the outward impression will be one of inconsistency.

A random or unstructured approach to process also means that businesses are potentially missing a trick. If the behaviour that leads to successful outcomes is not being fed back into - and replicated across - the wider organisation, the employees won't benefit from the chance to learn from each other, and the company will be rendered overly dependent on key individuals for their performance. If those people move on, results will suffer. Alternatively, if the business relies on mentoring to foster best practice, there is a risk that information becomes distorted as each different employee adds their own embellishments and perspectives on how things should operate.

To reliably scale success, businesses need to feed good practice into a replicable process.

It is quite striking to me that we can be so casual and parameter-less about something with such power to differentiate our business, when we are so attentive to how we maintain and protect customer data or financial information.

Even where business owners do try to document and provide templates for desired practice, these materials soon slide out of date, because process is – or should be - continuously evolving. And, more often than not, it is not the definitive best practice that is being captured, but rather an average experience that has been distilled from amid the inconsistency, or an amalgam of many diverse parts.

In the meantime, the way the business runs hardly changes. Managers may attempt to train people to behave in the documented way but with almost immediate effect people tend to revert to their old, comfortable approaches or in some other way deviate from the script.

The frustration for business owners, leaders and managers is palpable then, as they see jobs being performed in a sub-optimal way, and customer experiences and broader business outcomes being compromised. The temptation then might be to start meddling, trying to adjust what people are doing on a case-by-case basis. An endeavour which is ultimately unrewarding, and rarely successful. The owner/manager becomes jaded, while the individuals being targeted feel disempowered, criticised and demotivated. And actually their deviation isn't really their fault, because they haven't been given a process, structure or clear guidance to follow.

Is it any wonder we all suffer such work-related stress?!

Consistency cultivates confidence

Process matters because, if it is put together well and followed consistently across the organisation, it saves on all of the above. An evolving, living manual for success, a strong process provides a framework and structure for best behaviour and best outcomes. One that serves as both a handy reference tool and safety net, ensuring that everyone knows exactly what they should be doing, and how, at all times.

A finely-tuned process is critical to a business, and I believe its role in driving consistency is far more important - to everyone concerned (customers, employees and managers) – than achieving perfection. If you visit a premier hair salon and receive the haircut of your dreams five times in a row, then on the sixth time it's a disaster, you're unlikely to return because you can't rely on a consistent experience. By contrast if you have a consistently decent haircut at a no-frills local barber, always knowing what you'll get for your money, you'll be perfectly satisfied and much more likely to keep going back.

Just as, although Wagamama is nothing fancy, I like it as a place to eat because it never disappoints. It does what it does very well – every time – and this experience is reliably replicated at all of its branches.

"Consistency is far more important to customers and employees – and everybody, in fact – than perfection."

To explore more deeply why process matters, it's worth looking at some different aspects of a business and how the absence of consistent process, or the application of weak process, can have a detrimental impact. Below, I'll consider the bearing of poor process on everything from customer service and employee engagement, to operational efficiency and an organisation's financial health.

Strong process matters in all of these areas, but unfortunately this cannot always be counted upon.

Customer service

For most businesses, customer service is critical to commercial success. But delivering excellent customer service is by no means easy. Contrary to popular opinion, a good customer experience isn't guaranteed merely by having great staff, who are well trained, and incentivised to provide an optimal level of service.

As we've already established via a number of examples, most customers are really looking for a service that meets their needs *consistently* and *as expected*. And without strong process it is hard to guarantee that everybody, everywhere in the organisation, will provide this. The more that it is left to individuals to decide what an optimal experience looks like, and how to deliver it, the more variance there is likely to be. So that from day to day, or location to location, customers can never be quite sure what they will get. It's important to remember too that, what feels 'optimal' to one customer in one set of circumstances, may not feel optimal in a different scenario.

When I was setting up Process Bliss, we as a company commissioned a survey of a thousand people, asking how they perceived and experienced process in the business they worked for. (Rather than ask the managers, we felt it would be more valuable to get the view from the shop floor given that it's ultimately employees who see the full effects of process.) As many as 44 percent said they had seen their businesses lose clients due to poor internal processes. That's an astonishing figure, which shows the extent to which companies struggle to ensure the customer experience they aspire to.

Earlier, I talked about my experience with a hotel chain which saw me walk away from a brand I had loved - and spent an awful lot of money with - over a period of at least 15 years. A flaw in the company's process meant that staff couldn't treat me as an individual customer – one whose loyalty over the years had brought in a lot of income. When I had to cancel a booking three days before we were due to check in, they refused any scope for a refund. As a result of this negative experience, they lost my business – and any chance that I would recommend them again – forever.

Customers are even less tolerant of poor or inconsistent service when they interact with businesses online. As much as we suspect that consumers shop around primarily based on price, the evidence suggests that service factors such as reliable delivery, responsive and easy-to-navigate help, and a strong and consistent returns or cancellation policy rank much more highly in determining brand loyalty. Conversely, poor service is an immediate turn-off, especially when there are so many alternative online options to choose from.

Almost two-thirds of consumers (63 percent) say it only takes one unsatisfactory shopping experience to make them sever ties with a retail brand, according to BRP Consulting[4].

The ripples from a negative experience can be felt for a long time into the future. I bought some shoes from a bootmaker about 20 years ago. I had been shopping there for some five years before that: it's where I liked to buy all my shoes.

My last purchase however left a sour taste in my mouth, which to this day has stayed with me. I bought a pair of boots, but found immediately that there was a quality issue with them: the surface on the boots started to peel off. It was two weeks before I had an opportunity to go back to the shop to complain. I was told that I'd obviously done something to the boots to cause the problem, and that I wasn't entitled to a refund as I must have left them on a radiator or something! So, on top of an already disappointing brand experience, and the hassle of having to traipse back to the store to return the boots, I was accused of having caused this damage myself and refused a refund. This negative experience was so powerful that I vowed never to shop there again, and 20 years on, I still haven't.

Based on the frequency with which I had bought footwear from the brand previously, they have lost the sale of around 75 pairs of shoes since that

[4] Keeping Loyal Customers Happy, BRP Consulting, 2019.

fateful day. Failure to refund or replace that one pair of boots, worth £100, led to a loss of £7,500 in business over subsequent years. And that was just from one customer. Plus, I went on to tell my friends about the encounter.

"63 percent of consumers say it only takes one unsatisfactory shopping experience to make them severe ties with a retail brand."

Unless you're unique in your field, you won't be able to afford that kind of risk as a business. As many as 97 percent of consumers in the US confirm that bad customer service changes buying behaviour (compared with 87 percent who say the same for good customer service), and 46 percent say that changed behaviour still applies two years after a bad customer service experience[5].

This drives home the importance of providing the service customers expect 100 percent of the time – because all it takes is one bad experience to destroy years of hard-won loyalty and word-of-mouth brand kudos. It's why colossal global brands like Amazon plough so much into honing its customer experience, from its ever-growing portfolio of goods and services; personalised recommendations and even shoe size suggestions; ever more creative and convenient delivery options; and free product returns; to the chance to try out new clothing for a trial period before buying.

---

[5] Quantifying the business impact of customer service, Dimension Research, December 2018.

The company prides itself on being consistently good, and consistently better than alternative experiences. Everything is made easy for the customer: no need to re-enter account details, payment details, delivery preferences. No worries about what happens if something is faulty, ill-fitting or not as described. Even the smallest barriers to purchase have been eliminated.

Of course, one of Amazon's huge business differentiators is its use of advanced data analytics and process automation tools, which complete sophisticated sequences of tasks quickly and efficiently, while adapting experiences to each customer's preferences over time. The point being that it is process itself, and Amazon's continuous improvements to it, and the consistent service experience consumers have come to expect, that keeps customers coming back.

It isn't just in retail/consumer goods that a consistent, predictable customer experience matters, of course. The same applies in any field of business, from hospitality to the airline industry, and beyond. And in almost all - if not all - scenarios, it's the organisations with strong and clear values executed via robust, repeatable, documented process that win lasting loyalty – by doing what customers need and expect time after time after time.

We've already touched on hospitality, through my own personal experiences with hotels and restaurants. In the airline industry, research highlights the direct impact of prioritising systematic improvements to the customer experience. A study by Watermark found that airlines that had shown leadership here, backed by proactive investment in process improvements, saw their share value rise at more than double the rate of customer experience 'laggards' in the industry over a period of seven years.[6]

What's particularly interesting about the airline example is the sharp contrast, typically, in the application of process at the back end (operating aircraft: strong, robust, documented in detail, instinctively adhered to) versus the front end (customer service: patchy, random and all-too-readily abandoned when the heat is on).

When airline captain Chesley Burnett 'Sully' Sullenberger III successfully landed US Airways Flight 1549 in the Hudson River off Manhattan on January 15, 2009, after both engines were disabled by a bird strike, it was thanks to his quick thinking and automatic application of emergency protocol that the plane came down safely and all 155 people aboard survived.

It would be unthinkable not to have clear, robust, documented processes for ensuring airline safety and emergency responses. Yet when it comes to looking after passengers in all other ways, airline processes are often hit and miss – from poor customer communication around live schedule issues, to inconsistent service on board, to sketchy after-care in the event of late or cancelled services.

---

[6] The Customer Experience ROI Study (Airline Industry Edition), Watermark Consulting, 2019.

An airline might have the best safety record in the industry, but if no one wants to fly with them because of inadequate customer service process, the brand outcome will be poor.

Employee engagement, motivation & loyalty

Employees like to know what they are doing, and how to perform their jobs well. Documented process helps them to do that with confidence. When process is weak, inconsistent or largely absent, and too much is left to chance, it can have a detrimental effect on motivation because people are never quite sure how they are doing.

Our own research shows that 33 percent of employees have taken time off due to work-related stress and 42 percent have gone so far as to change jobs due to frustrations at work. These are alarmingly high numbers. When we started to drill down into what was going on behind the scenes, we discovered two seemingly contradictory forces at work. One was that people were not being given sufficient guidance on how to do their jobs well; the other was that managers were continuously chasing and checking up on employees, in effect micro-managing them. These two issues sit at opposite extremes of a spectrum. People don't want to be dropped in it with no support, nor do they want to be micromanaged. The fact is most people want to sit somewhere in between and if they find themselves at those extremes they become unhappy.

Generally, people don't leave employment for a better salary. More usually it's because they are being ground down where they are, feeling that their talents are not being put to good use or fully appreciated, and/or that their employer is not supporting them to be their best.

To excel and thrive, people need guidance and a clearly set-out process to follow. They need to understand the rules of play, the preferred approach; the desired outcomes and how best to achieve them. They need training – something to help them to do their job well, and parameters to guide them. Unless they understand what good looks like, they will have nothing to measure their own performance by. If someone is on the right track, it is helpful for them to understand and feel this so they can continue in the right direction and keep improving.

By giving people a process, as an employer or manager, you are supporting them to do a good job – by helping them understand exactly what's expected of them, and how they can shine. Better still, once staff have clear guidelines to work from, they become more self-sufficient. That is, it is less necessary for managers or business owners to check up on them. Employees then feel trusted, empowered and engaged in their work, which continues to drive up performance - and so the cycle of positive motivation and mood becomes self-perpetuating.

I learned this myself from personal experience. When I was running my previous business, eShare, and first started to develop Process Bliss (software to manage processes, which led to my current company), I created a first version of the software product that was quite controlling. My goal was to create a basic product that would encapsulate a process, along with clear guidance and documents for employees to follow. It would allow different people to complete different steps, and tick these off as they completed them – while crucially also providing scope for employees to explain why they may not have been able to complete some steps.

When we developed and launched the software, I was quite busy meddling in my business and checking up on everybody, and making sure things were being done the way I wanted them to be. I *thought* I wanted to see reports of everything that was being done and anything that wasn't. But actually, with a solid process in place, this ceased to be necessary. I learned that once people are equipped with all the tools they need to do a good job, they don't need overt supervision.

Assuming employees have bought into the process (*more on this later*), and can see the benefits of it, they will start to take ownership of it. This in turn invites a new level of trust and reassurance. People want to be able to deliver something they can be proud of, which means they are likely to proactively report any issues with the process. So, as a manager, you're able to leave them to it. Before long, everything is running like clockwork, and the manager or business owner is free to focus on higher-level decision-making.

If process is implemented correctly, it should be possible to see status updates about how everything is going, removing the need for managers to keep chasing teams or individuals for updates – which in itself can cause stress (it was the third most common cause of employee demotivation in our research).

In a positive, process-enabled scenario, keeping key people in the loop should feel instinctive, because everyone desires – and wants to be seen to be working towards - the same outcome: success.

Securing investment

When selling your business or securing investment, strong process is ranked as the second most important factor after the finances. Having demonstrable strong processes in all areas of the business is a key factor in determining whether you receive the funding or make the sale.

To give you an example, if you've ever sold a business you'll have found it a fascinating experience.

When I was selling my previous business eShare, we agreed the sale via a Letter of Intent and we started a thorough round of due diligence.

I had always imagined this would be a matter of providing gigabytes of data and documentation. Whilst unfortunately my expectations were by no means let down in that department there was a more interesting and enjoyable phase where the purchaser flew a team of 20 people over to London from New York and we spent two full days in a hotel meeting room with my team of six and all the advisors. The objective seemed to be to grill my team about how they worked and their processes. This involved the head of their various departments, finance, HR, operations, development etc interviewing their respective counterparts within my team.

We kicked off talking about the finances of the business and my Head of Finance and I were being asked how we performed various financial processes. This included our monthly billing, production of management accounts, payroll, debtor chasing and regulatory returns amongst other things.

The purchasers wanted to hear from the horse's mouth that these processes were well thought through, well known and well embedded within the team and that everyone involved understood what they needed to do.

As they started asking these questions whilst listening, I logged onto our software platform Process Bliss and showed them the processes in action.

All 20 people struggled to grasp what they were looking at and their initial reaction was "no, no, no we don't want to see the documentation, we know you've probably got that, what we want to know is that you guys are on top of it and that you are performing these things well so we would rather just talk to you." To which our response was "this isn't documentation this is the process. Our processes aren't managed by 5 different people all storing different bits in their head. Our processes are a living entity and they are there to support our people. What you're looking at isn't documentation; this is the live system. What you see is, where we are with these processes , their current status, who has done what and when, along with the proof and what is due next.

I'll talk more about this later in the book.

As they realised what they were staring at there was this wonderful moment when about 2/3rds of the people in the room suddenly stood up and walked towards the projector screen. As it dawned on them that they were looking at a live view of our whole business they started to smile.

For the rest of the two days as we ran through department by department, again and again we showed them how our business was run by showing them the live processes.

The reassurance that this transparent view, almost proof that the business was run in such a robust, clockwork way was living proof that their purchase was a good one and helped to reassure the purchasers that they were taking minimal risk.

As a more specific example, when you sell a business, as a founder and owner there is a lot of emotion attached, and deals can be quite fragile if the sales process isn't tightly managed according to a strong, proven process which covers all bases.

A month or so later during the sale, there was a sudden make-or-break point just a couple of weeks before signing all the paperwork. We'd supplied a wealth of information about the company, but as part of the due diligence process the buyer had asked whether any of our client contracts had certain clauses in them, including a "termination for convenience" clause.

A major source of the value of eShare's business was its recurring client revenues. However, sometimes, clients ask for a clause that would allow them to terminate the contract at any point in time. It was reasonable, then, that the purchaser would want to know how prevalent such clauses were across our client base.

Although it was unfortunate that we had not anticipated the request for this information when collating data for the purchasers, the greater issue was that when we started eShare we had never thought to make a record of any special clauses that had been agreed, as part of our process for bringing new clients on board. With hindsight, our onboarding process would have recorded these clauses in a spreadsheet or database.

Our typical contract was approximately 14 pages long and at the time I sold the business we had about 700 clients, so to look up all of this information retrospectively was a considerable undertaking.

Our process oversight meant that, at a crucial point in the company's sale, when emotions were running high and we were at a point of negotiating over little things, someone suddenly had to make the time to check through nearly 10,000 pages of contracts looking for termination-for-convenience clauses. This led to some considerable stress, not least as the delay incurred could have cost us the deal.

Fortunately, the transaction still went ahead but the experience highlights the risks of an insufficient process. I might have lost the sale, and our financial advisor his commission. All for the sake of a subtle, overlooked administrative step that would have cost little or nothing to include upfront if only we had thought to.

Indeed, it's often the smallest details that create operational interruptions or inefficiency.

A friend of mine runs a car franchise, with three forecourts located in different parts of the same city. He let off some steam one day when we were together watching a cricket match, complaining that his job seemed to be largely taken up with making sure 'everyone' does 'everything', 'every' time. "It's amazing how difficult that seems to be," he sighed.

It must have been exhausting too. I asked him for an example of where process was letting him down and the impact that could have. It boiled down to the checks the company had to conduct when buying a car off somebody – to ensure there is no debt associated with it, which the business would then become liable for.

"If we buy a car for £5,000, and it's got £2,000 of debt against it, ultimately that means that we have to repay that £2,000," he explained. "If that happens, we can resolve it, because we can go back to the person who sold us the car and we reclaim that money off them. But that's an incredibly time-consuming process, and it means we're stuck with the car on our forecourt because it can't be sold in the meantime."

Performing the HPI (hire purchase insurance) checks was a quick and simple online task to ensure there was no debt, but staff were forgetting or neglecting to do them because it was so rare that the cars they were purchasing carried any debt. But for every one in 10 cases where there *was* an issue, the forgotten check wreaked havoc – tying up space on the forecourt while creating laborious admin, and in the worst cases resulting in a loss when vehicles were sold on.

Hindsight is a wonderful thing. When my friend set up his business and performed his first vehicle history check this would have been an ideal time to build this into the car purchase process. But just implementing this into a purchase process at any point would have fixed the problem once and for all. However the solution he had found was not to have a great process but to keep manually checking himself that people were performing this activity and reprimanding them if they didn't. This was exhausting him and no doubt it did little for the motivation of his brow beaten employees.

Far better to learn and adapt to a hard lesson once, than to keep repeating the same mistake. As I'll discuss in more detail later, it's important for any process to be adaptable and for there to be a feedback loop so that as each new issue presents itself (and they will), the process can be improved.

As my father used to say, "Make a mistake once and you're human; make the same mistake again and you're a fool."

Continuous learning and adaptation is what will give your business a persistent edge over its competitors.

Maximising leaders' time

A sign of a good business leader or manager is someone who makes themselves redundant - certainly in day-to-day operations. Once you have put in place the right mechanisms and support systems to ensure everything can run smoothly and to plan, you should be able to spend the majority of your time on looking where to take the business next.

Yet too many business owners get drawn into maintaining the status quo. That's what was happening to my friend with the car dealerships, and is something I have experienced first-hand in my previous business. We see things being done in a sub-optimal way, and we can't help but get involved.

And very soon, things start to spiral out of control. The doubt sets in and you begin thinking, "Well, if that pricing wasn't updated on the website, what else is inaccurate?" Before long, you've become an auditor and hands-on supervisor - your role has become Head of Policing Quality - there to spot things that are going wrong and bring them back on course - as though that's the way you will improve and grow the business.

On a practical level, this causes two problems. The first is that it takes up time you can ill afford, when there are far better ways you can spend your time to improve your business. The second is that you're essentially creating a culture of mistrust if you are continuously checking up on people, ready to correct their mistakes or point out their inadequacies. This is a soul-destroying scenario for everyone concerned, and will eventually lead to good people leaving. Employees who feel they are being monitored with an expectation of failure will soon feel disempowered and demotivated, increasingly becoming less engaged and less loyal. As they continue to care steadily less and less, your problems multiply.

Our own research suggests that more than half of senior managers in small to medium enterprises lose a day of their week to simply checking up on and managing process; a third waste as much as two days of their week on this kind of policing activity. This is a key issue for business owners and CEOs – and yet such an easy problem to fix. It comes back to refining the process and guidance provided to employees so that they can confidently deliver what's expected, consistently, every time.

Homing in on individual failings and addressing them will feel like death by a thousand cuts. The problem is much more likely to be systemic, the solution being one of strengthened, documented process – a framework and structure to support people in doing their best work, in the way you expect and hope it will be done.

"Home in on individual failings and addressing them will feel like death by a thousand cuts."

In the introduction to this book, I alluded to my own experiences of being a 'helicopter' manager (hovering over everyone, keeping everyone's movements within my sight) when I headed up my previous company, eShare. Having built the business from scratch, I saw it as something precious and potentially perfect. I really wanted my customers to be happy and I wanted our product to be amazing. I wanted to deliver a fantastic service.

There was nothing wrong with having big aspirations for the company. But, as we got bigger, we started to hire people who, although they cared and wanted to do a good job, didn't necessarily have the same zeal and all-consuming commitment that I had to making everything perfect. It wasn't that they didn't want to do a great job; rather that they had a life outside the office and arguably a healthier perspective on work than I perhaps did.

But it wasn't only that, they also had different views on how things should be done and in my passion for perfection I struggled to recognise this. This meant their great ideas for new ways of working often were overlooked or worse rebutted. When this happened we lost an opportunity to improve.

Every business needs diversity, and people with different opinions. But it can be hard to let go of control when you're used to everything being and happening a certain way. So at first my reaction was to maintain vigilance, poised as a quality controller to point out the small errors of people's ways, the niggling little things they had overlooked or not quite done to my standards. And of course the more I looked, the more faults I found.

I was effectively filling the gaps left by my team and taking responsibility away from them. In so doing, I was creating more work for myself, and signalling to my staff that I didn't really trust them. By watching over them, ready to point out their next mistake, I was robbing them of their chance to shine, or even to learn from their own errors. I was lucky I didn't lose anyone; I must have made a few people's lives a misery.

Eventually it dawned on me that my approach was not sustainable; that perhaps there was a common theme behind the issues I was encountering – and that the issue was more something I had not done: *ie* show the way with a manual for how to excel in the jobs that needed to be done – a clearly set-out process, documented in a way that people could easily understand, work from and check against.

Of course I am far from the only owner/manager who has had to rein themselves in and stop trying to control everything across their growing business, and as a consequence making poor use of their time.

A guy I know runs a window double-glazing business. His business model is fairly simple. He advertises which brings in leads, then a salesperson visits the customer's house to measure up, extol the benefits of double-glazing, and provide a quote. The customer then signs a contract and pays a deposit. The two parties schedule the work and, over a period of days, the new windows are installed. After which the company bills for the balance.

It's not a particularly complex business and there are people to run all the departments – advertising, sales, operations. Yet the guy at the helm works 18 hours a day.

Now, the vision for the business is well-defined: everything is in place so it should just run itself. Yet the business owner too often finds himself drawn into the day-to-day detail, the microscopic elements that, to his perfectionist mind, aren't quite right.

It might be that when a sale is agreed, the customer has been promised something the installation manager can't deliver, which in turn leads to the customer being unhappy. With a good strong process to prevent those issues arising, the business owner would be able to take more of a back seat. But, without those safety measures, the head of the company felt he couldn't afford to take his eye off the ball.

A proper process is the key to freedom for the micro-manager. It will help you reclaim your time and use your energy more productively where it is really needed.

Keeping the cash flowing

It's critical to any business and its cash flow that its finances are run efficiently. If you don't have good processes in place, things can quickly unravel.

Take debt collection. There are likely to be some variables at play. For instance, if an invoice hasn't been paid it may be because the customer isn't happy and has a justifiable complaint. And if you're too heavy-handed in your approach to chasing payment, you may risk losing a customer. This can also create the wrong impression for your business, if you are perceived as caring more about getting the money than in looking after your customers and providing a great service.

As a potentially sensitive activity, debt collection needs to be approached in a particular way. If you leave this up to individuals to gauge, it may lead to friction – not least because the fallout will extend far beyond Finance. Service delivery teams may become involved, for instance, if the customer has some sort of complaint and that's why they haven't paid their bill.

Yet, remarkably, many businesses leave the debt collection process to chance – how it is handled depends on who is in the hot seat on the day. Perhaps it won't even register as a priority, because of time pressure.

I've seen this happen – not in my business, but elsewhere. A business owner, bringing in a CEO so he could start to take a less hands-on role, found to his horror that the new chief immediately let go the financial clerk and hired a finance director. Within two months, debt collection had ground to a halt and the company's debts had nearly tripled. The poor business owner found himself drawn back into the everyday running of the company, sending the CEO off to pastures new.

The issue had been that the company's process for recouping unpaid bills was known only to the financial clerk. So when that person left, the new financial employees had to develop their own processes – which clearly were not effective.

Paying staff

For obvious reasons, it's important to have great processes in place for paying your employees reliably and on time – failure to do this will create employee dissatisfaction, suggesting to them that they are not valued and potentially causing problems and stress in their personal lives if they cannot meet their own financial commitments. To avoid sensitive fallouts due to payroll errors, and ensure salaries and wages are paid correctly and on time every time, you need a robust process to follow. Larger companies may use specialist external payroll services to pay people, but again this fundamentally relies on strong processes being in place to ensure that nothing is overlooked – from overtime and expenses, to pay rises resulting from a promotion.

Management reporting: keeping all parts of the business in the loop

A systematic plan for preparing and putting together management accounts is critical too, yet it's surprising how many businesses approach this as a novel experience each time.

Producing reliable management accounts is no easy feat, but these reports are essential to informing next steps and decisions about the business. And for each department and team, it's important that people can flick straight to the insights that affect them the most. So creating management reports in a predictable and easily digestible format, and distributing the right data to the right people in the right part of the business, needs strong processes.

It's a misconception that management accounts are really just a profit and loss statement prepared for directors to review. For a business to keep improving, everyone in the company needs to know where performance is strongest and weakest, and where improvements can be made.

For instance, sales teams will need information on revenue performance, where money hasn't been collected, or if there has been subsequent customer comeback about a product or service. The customer services function may want insight into how many clients have upgraded their products or bought additional wraparound services. The HR and payroll teams, meanwhile, will need information to update their records and calculate commission and bonuses for staff that have met targets or exceeded expectations.

It tends to be here, in the drilled-down detail, that any process around management accounts tends to fall down. There may be no issue with creating an accurate set of figures at the end of each period, but distributing actionable insights to those beyond the top team can be too random and ad-hoc, leading to frustration as sales managers, HR/payroll personnel, or other departments are forced to chase the information they need.

This frustration can lead to broader friction, a cultural divide between 'them' and 'us'. For instance, a sales department may consider the finance team to be useless because it isn't confirming sales figures in time to ensure commission is paid when due. The finance department, in turn, may be bad mouthing sales for neglecting to routinely provide the data needed for correct P&L forecasting.

An agreed, documented process that everyone buys into could transform this situation, by keeping information flowing systematically through the business to where it needs to be, complete, and in the right format, at the time it is needed.

"A systematic plan for preparing and putting together management accounts is critical, yet it's surprising how many businesses approach this as a novel experience each time."

Process – particularly if you use software to manage it – allows you to ensure that all the relevant stakeholders play their part in the smooth financial management of the business.

Take our invoicing process at my previous company, eShare. Managing this efficiently and reliably relied on data from the sales teams on what had been purchased; customer services on whether a system had been deployed, to enable billing; and the IT department on system and data usage. Once we had all this data, we could start to collate it in the financial system to produce the invoices. In certain cases, invoices also needed to be checked, and potentially modified.

End to end, this process involved multiple departments. To keep operations slick and robust, we applied simple but effective process software. This set out a series of steps, each assigned to someone specific, with a date each month when the given task needed to be performed. Every month, the individual was assigned this step and knew when they had to perform it. If they needed to provide data, they would attach this to the task in the system and mark it as completed. Then the next person was notified, and logged in to fulfil their part of the process. And so it went on.

Everyone had a clear, transparent view of the overall process, so they knew where they stood. They could see what their particular responsibility was within the process. They were also kept up to date as colleagues completed and ticked off their respective tasks, and were provided with the data they needed to perform their own steps – all in one central place, where they could also access any document templates they needed, and guidance in how to handle exceptions/special cases.

Documenting everything and providing a mechanism by which we performed the work brought shape and rhythm to the invoicing process, for all concerned. Although implementing the new system was no mean feat, once this was in place it was almost impossible to imagine how we managed without the discipline of the process software.

For instance, previously, if someone had been absent, or for some other reason neglected to do their part, the whole invoicing process was potentially held up by days, weeks or even months. Errors would creep in, too – resulting in unhappy customers if overbilled; loss of revenue if we had under-billed; or a delay in collecting revenue because we hadn't been able to get the invoices out of the door.

The point is that strong process is fundamental to business: without it, even a solid operation can go under. Consider how often even the most ostensibly successful organisations go into administration due to spiralling cash flow issues – all because the business lost control of process. By contrast, great process can liberate companies to excel and thrive, because these businesses are running a tight ship and continuously refining their processes to support sustainable growth and controlled innovation.

"Strong process is fundamental to business: without it, even a solid operation can go under."

Later in this book, we'll look at some of the human failings that can lead to poor or inconsistent process adoption, and establish how – through inclusive collaboration – you can create processes that people will willingly follow, without feeling controlled and/or that the prescribed steps are a burden. I will show you how, once you have done this successfully, you will be able to take a big step back - liberating yourself from the feeling that you must continuously monitor what teams are doing, because you know staff now have the tools they need to do a great job.

I'm also going to explain how to make your new approach to 'process' something that your employees will love – because it will make their jobs so much simpler, and because you're also going to give employees a voice and empower them so that if an agreed process feels wrong, or isn't working efficiently, they can say so and start to improve it.

As part of all this, we're going to harness the collaborative power of your team. So, that as your people start to proactively provide input, and see their suggested improvements take effect, *every* employee in your business begins to help improve the way your business operates - so that you don't have to. You will find that collectively they are better at it than you could ever imagine and far far better at it than you - trust me.

What's more, we're going to make this fun.

5

THE PROBLEM

Within any business, there are really two overarching sets of processes. There are the ones that management think are being performed. These are often sitting in a file somewhere and are brought out occasionally for training purposes or when things go wrong.

Then, of course, there is what actually happens day to day. More often than not, this bears little resemblance to what's in the manual.

The 5 reasons process fails

Let's go back to that common scenario just mentioned, where a document setting out the desired process lies tucked away in a file, in a drawer or on a shared server. Someone took the time and effort to put this together, but in practice it is rarely looked at. Perhaps the document is updated once a year, in an attempt to bring it into line with every-day reality. But this is even more absurd when you think about it, given that everything is supposed to flow from the documented process, and not the other way round.

Documenting a process is merely about creating a formal record of what should be happening routinely across the organisation. It is a supporting reference guide, in case of query. All you're really doing by capturing a process in words - and perhaps diagrams or a video - is cementing what's already been agreed and which should by now be instinctive routine.

But all too often there is a gap between intention and what's delivered, or between what the management thinks is being done, and the way people are actually operating.

There are five main reasons why process fails:

1. People have great ideas/think they know better
2. People have ***not*** so great ideas/think they know better
3. People forget things
4. CBA (people 'can't be arsed')
5. Miscommunication ('Nobody told me').

Let's delve deeper into each of these.

1. Great ideas

When James A. Champy and Michael Hammer wrote their original book[7] on *Reengineering the Corporation,* one of the standout claims they made is that processes need to be owned by the individuals who operate them. If not, they are likely to veer their own way in any case. And this makes good sense. People are much more likely to believe in and buy into a process if they feel ownership of it and have some input into it. So if they have great ideas, why not incorporate them into the process? If they are the ones adhering to it every day, they're probably in a better position than you are

[7] Reengineering the Corporation: A Manifesto for Business Revolution, James A. Champy, Michael Martin Hammer, 1993.

to know what works and also what's less effective or inefficient (which in turn may be making them miserable).

You want to manage the business, and you don't want people's creativity to be dampened. The trouble is that sometimes your employees' great ideas aren't exactly what you want. Maybe there's something in their suggestions that make sense, but throwing out everything that has gone before feels too drastic.

The ideal would be to sort their better ideas from the weaker ones, and then merge only the best aspects of those ideas into your chosen process, rather than ignoring them altogether or allowing staff to go rogue (which can be tempting to keep them happy, and allow them to show flair and initiative). Great ideas are a positive thing: if they are not harnessed at all this will lead to frustration. But boundaries are important too.

2. Not-so-great ideas

Giving people the freedom to stray from the process often makes them stray in a direction you don't want them to go. They may undermine, ignore a step or bypass/eliminate a part of the process that is really important to you as a business, but doesn't seem important to them because they're coming at it from a different perspective.

Their intentions, and ideas for improvement, may not be the best, but ignoring initiative can backfire. Certainly, you want to avoid creating chaos. But I strongly believe that something can be learned from almost every suggestion or idea, and that the only stupid question is the one that isn't asked. So hear out - and look for a positive angle to - all ideas, even if you can't carry them forward.

"Something can be learned from almost every suggestion or idea; the only stupid question is the one that isn't asked."

3. Forgetfulness

People forget. With any kind of process, there are likely to be multiple steps involved. Rather than document the steps that most people will need to take, we try to store them in our heads, and then we pass these stored processes around from one person to another over time. We then expect everybody to get it all right. When they don't, we blame and criticise them.

This is a common source of frustration for business owners/managers, and of employee demotivation which leads to workplace stress. As humans we're creative, and if we feel engaged at work it's natural to come up with inspired ideas and want to implement them so we can shine. What we're not so great at is remembering to do 20 things, consistently, without ever missing a step, time and time again.

So it's quite handy that we live in a digital age, where computer programs and apps can do all of this for us – serving up reminders and prompts, supporting staff at hectic times when their minds might go blank, with a motivational and reassuring checklist they can check tasks off against. And if they want a paper copy to have in their hands, that's easily provided too.

Even where staff have been with the company a long time, they may still have trouble remembering changes to processes, as systems are honed and tweaked and updated to reflect new requirements, or in response to employee or customer feedback.

And of course a process may be multi-faceted, involving five different departments doing 40 things. This all has to work perfectly, and everybody along the chain has to remember how they're supposed to communicate with all the other departments.

Is it any wonder that people get in a mess and tensions are created between different departments, as they vent their frustrations and look for someone to blame for any perceived inefficiency? This is very unfortunate, and unfair, as humans – especially busy ones, with a lot on their plates - will always forget things. Rather than force the impossible – perfection by rote – wouldn't it make more sense to provide people with the tools to support them in getting the process right?

There is another dimension to this as well. Sometimes process is more complicated than just a linear series of steps. A process might also involve documents, data, customers and suppliers, and interplay between them – such as getting correct data to the sales team, so that they can get the correct data off the customer, so that the operations team can do their job. Or the operations team capturing the correct data so that finance can progress with billing.

All this complicates things even further. In most businesses, we still require humans to perform these processes, yet we're not providing systematic help to them as they do it. We issue all the instructions, and expect them to get on with it - then criticise when they don't do it right. And we wonder why people often dread coming to work!

4. The 'can't be arsed' (CBA) contingent

With any process, there will always be dissenters: those who deliberately decide they're not going to perform a particular step of the process which they believe to be superfluous or tedious. You've explained that it's important, made this very clear, and trained them how to do it. However you haven't convinced them that they actually *need* to execute that particular task, so it seems perfectly justifiable to them not to bother.

Again, this is a human problem. People develop workarounds to get jobs done more efficiently, especially if they are pushed for time. But, more often than not, it's because they haven't truly appreciated (or been told) *why* it needs to be done, that they conveniently skip a step. They cannot see the bigger picture, because no one has taken the time to paint this for them.

The solution to this begins with being more transparent about the overall process, why it exists and why it has been designed in a certain way. Understanding the wider context can change their perception and bring them into line, of their own volition.

Take the sales team at a double-glazing business, which have been asked to capture some very detailed information about the exact components of the wall where a new window is going to be installed (such as make, size and unusual features). Taking down all of these details time after time might seem excessive, especially when the answers are the same in 99 percent of cases. But if a step is skipped, and the measurements differ on one occasion, the operation team might turn up with the wrong windows, wasting everyone's time and causing considerable expense.

The cost of asking the questions was next to nothing, whereas the 'lazy' shortcut could cost a company hundreds or even thousands of pounds, depending on the situation. It may result in a delayed job, surplus stock, a delay while reordering supplies, and the need to return with different equipment on a separate day (delaying other jobs), while risking losing custom and gaining a bad reputation. No one wants those consequences on their shoulders, so it's always worth explaining why every step in a process matters to get everyone on board.

5. 'Nobody told me'

The 'Nobody told me' scenario, which can sound a lot like someone not taking responsibility for doing what's expected of them, is typically the result of miscommunication. While there may be a process in the file, it could be that this isn't being referred to when a job is done. Or that people don't refer to a documented process because it's gone astray or doesn't exist. Perhaps the preferred way to do the job may be recorded only in people's heads, and/or is something that has evolved gradually over time – so that the filed version is a few iterations behind, and has yet to catch up.

These are all risky scenarios, because they rely on those who do the job every day in a way that has been perfected over time, remembering to pass on their knowledge to others who may have to step into their shoes at some point – especially if this is without warning, because the main person is off sick. Too much is being left to chance, with high potential that the wheels will come off at some point.

Process erosion

Without clear guidelines that are updated and communicated routinely, processes can be steadily eroded over time. The most common scenario where this happens is when one employee leaves and a new person joins, requiring a knowledge transfer from Employee A to Employee B. This transition will never be perfect. If we were computers, we would be able to download and transfer the process file from Brain A to Brain B, without any data loss. But as we are human, knowledge transfer will only ever be partial.

In all likelihood, the whole process won't be completely explained or, even if it is and it's explained well, the recipient may not interpret what's being communicated in the way it was intended, influenced by their own experiences and previous ways of working. And so things begin to slip off course, and standards are gradually watered down. Without the right controls in place, this could undermine everything you've worked hard to achieve. Over time, and as more people move in and out of roles, the situation will continue to spiral. It becomes like a complex game of Chinese Whispers.

The cornerstone of great scalable businesses is consistency. The most successful brands in the world are not those with the sharpest logo, but those which offer a particular experience which customers appreciate and know they can rely on. That could be product quality, attentive after-sales service, or friendly and courteous staff in every store. Similarly, employees will often rate a company based on how well it is run and how well supported they are to do a good job every day.

The same is true of your suppliers, your partners, and even those who don't have first-hand experience of your business. They will build up an image of the company, what you stand for, what you're good at. Just as children thrive on consistency to feel safe and that they can count on something or someone, the same is true as we become adults and venture out into the world. Consistency means that everyone knows where they stand and what to expect. It gives people a framework within which to operate confidently.

Inter-departmental communications

If a single person, or department, comes up with and implements the perfect process, that's all well and good. But if that behaviour stops at the door, and equivalent experiences are not reflected across the business, there will be no consistency – for customers, for employees whose role may traverse departmental lines, or for third parties dealing with different parts of the company.

And often processes themselves will involve people across the business playing their role to deliver the complete end-to-end experience. This requires collaboration and access to shared process documentation. Yet, in most complex organisations, silos, conflicting agendas, and poor communications can hamper a consistent end-to-end experience every time.

Take my old company, eShare. Whenever we brought a new customer on board, Sales would be involved in making sure the client was happy with the service we were going to provide, managing expectations, and ensuring they signed the contract. Then they would hand over to Customer Services, who would be responsible for training clients, bringing them up to speed, and making sure that all their employees were able to use our software. Finance would need to collect data to enable us to bill and some of this data would come from various sources at various stages of the project. Marketing might get involved next, to see if satisfied customers might be willing to take part in a case study or some other publicity. So there were multiple parties within the business each liaising with the customer in turn, to deliver the complete experience across the customer account lifecycle.

Processes can be incredibly complex, depending on the scale and nature of the business. There might be outside resources that are imported in. There may be other parties, such as suppliers, who have to be factored in. Managing all of this can be very challenging.

We've already looked at five common reasons why process can fail in any business. With more complex processes, the scope for converging issues and the likelihood of process failure are even higher. More often than not, this is because multiple departments or entities are involved.

Inevitably, if process failure occurs this will cause friction at some point, typically with the client becoming unhappy. When a customer is unhappy, they will make complaints to the sales department, the implementation team, and the customer support team. When a complaint comes in, it is escalated, and people start to look at what went wrong.

Typically, the underlying problem is a breakdown in communication between departments. This can result in much finger-pointing - which is generally very unhelpful - and cultural tension as two or more teams are set against each other. And because they are not supporting each other, this does little to help resolve the issues. And so the negative cycle continues.

So, getting process right is rarely a simple case of setting down and agreeing some rules about how things should be done. In larger organisations with complex departments, it can become a bit of a minefield, creating stresses within the business.

At eShare, there was a lot to get right. Our software product was being used by about 20,000 senior board members of major companies, charities, universities, hospitals, and other institutions. They were all accessing our servers to use our software for putting together and distributing papers for board meetings.

These high-ranking users expected very high levels of service and didn't like it if things didn't work. So, when we deployed updates to our software, good communication between our various departments was essential. Customer support had to be properly trained in advance, so they fully understood what the new features were, what issues might arise, how clients might react, what their actions might be, and how to deal with these responses. If the customer service team wasn't able to manage all of this appropriately, the result would have been unhappy customers.

Similarly, sales also needed to be aware of all the new features. If sales agents were unaware of the specific updates, it risked embarrassment during the sales demonstrations if they were unable to answer customers' questions. The same applied to marketing, whose job was to communicate the new features both to existing clients and prospective customers. If they failed to do this, we would have been missing out on an opportunity to highlight our improved competitive advantage, to win new business and keep existing customers engaged and loyal.

All of this relied on a robust and consistent process to make sure that people were kept informed about what was coming, what they needed to do and when they needed to do it. There was nothing inherently difficult about this. But in too many businesses this kind of thing isn't done systematically or well, leading to unnecessary tension and stress.

A friend of mine runs a consultancy business, which has been expanding very quickly. Something it is very good at is recruitment – thanks to its emphasis on *talent* rather than years of experience when appointing new people to roles.

There have been lots of studies done on this. If you recruit based on *experience,* you'll typically have a 25 percent success rate, whereas if you recruit based on *talent,* that rate will soar to 75 percent. If you look at the make-up of people when you are recruiting them, there are typically five distinct elements that determine their potential desirability or suitability for a role:

- Talent – a person's intelligence or talent;
- Values – what's fundamentally important to an individual;
- Motivation – what drives a person's behaviour;
- Behaviour – how a person acts and behaves;
- Experience – what a person has done.

Of these five qualities, experience is probably the easiest to change. This is because you can *give* people experience. Behaviour isn't that hard to alter. Motivation is harder, but still possible. Values are nearly impossible to change. Intelligence and talent though are what you're born with, and that's that!

It's interesting, then, that so many organisations recruit based on a candidate's experience rather than their talent or intelligence. My friend's consultancy sought to challenge this paradigm. But this required strong process to ensure that talented people were adequately supported to successfully deliver results.

The business owner had designed the recruitment process from start to finish with great attention to detail, and business had got off to a great start, bringing in some very talented people. Yet the process for staff on-boarding was faltering.

My friend had put a lot of thought into how the company would make its people happy. When someone new joined, certain things were supposed to happen. On their first day at work, someone would have found out what their favourite biscuits were, and put a packet of them on their desk, for example.

New joiners would also be given more of an insight into the business. This included going through a document (known as a playbook) with the CEO, who would explain the vision and values of the business - why it existed, how it planned to succeed, how it stood apart from its competitors, and its short, medium and long-term goals.

Alignment is crucial in any business, ensuring that everyone in an organisation is on the same page. Everybody knows where they are heading and how to make decisions, because they understand the drivers of the business, why it exists and what's needed for it to succeed.

Yet it turned out that at my friend's consultancy, the playbook walkthrough was not happening consistently. My friend began to look at how to improve the process to address this. When we discussed the issue, she became quite animated, adamant that she now wanted to see a report confirming that every employee joining had been through the playbook. Doubt had set in, and she wanted proof that something very important to her was happening routinely.

But when we drilled down a bit deeper, we discovered that the real issue was that my friend had lost faith in her team's ability or desire to follow a process she had created with good reason. She then started to worry about what other elements of the process had slipped, her natural response being to try to put additional controls in place to bring everyone back on course. Over time, people had been changing the processes, dropping steps and bypassing best practices.

The risk here was that, in becoming focused on specifics, my friend had lost sight of far more important elements of the employee on-boarding process, such as financial and criminal record checks. The other danger was staff would resist additional controls, and feel demotivated that these were being put in place.

Putting in process software proved the solution. It gave everyone clear guidelines to follow and check against in a non-threatening context, and it allowed my friend to step back and trust that process would be followed consistently. Very soon, the business was back on track and my friend could relax again.

Process promotes productivity

Process is crucial to the success and smooth-running of a business, to the point that it's the second thing private equity firms look at after the finances in determining a company's prospects and value. Without great customer acquisition and retention processes, there won't be a reliable income. And without great processes to find, hire and retain staff, who will deliver an exceptional product and service to customers?

We have already identified that one of the major causes of work-related stress is either too much process, or a lack of process leading to people not knowing what to do. But when poorly applied process also leads to managers and CEOs continuously checking up on and micromanaging staff, this is also a failure.

And one of the first things to suffer is productivity. As we have already noted, your business's ability to continuously deliver its financial health, and its degree of operational waste are all directly affected by process. Yet, particularly here in the UK, we treat formalised process with disdain – with one rule for 'data' (treated with utmost vigilance and rigour) and another for 'operational knowledge and instruction' (mostly arbitrary, rarely documented).

Associations with rules, control and dehumanisation in the workplace have tainted perceptions of process. People instinctively think of it as something imposed, something which removes the scope for initiative and free thought. And how can individuals shine if everyone is working from the same rigid instruction manual?

But too much freedom can be paralysing. Just as busy, organised people can become lost without a list to refer to, a business which lets its people 'wing it' risks chaos and even personal stress, because they have no reassuring structure to guide them when they lose their way, become overloaded or face a crisis situation. Paramedics or 'crash-cart' medical teams responding to emergencies where every minute lost to indecision could be a matter of life and death, or an airline pilot like 'Sully' who must suddenly react under extreme pressure, would be lost without a well-rehearsed process – the emergency drill – to refer to.

Yet in everyday business practice, too many people eschew process, believing it inhibits their creativity and ability to differentiate themselves. This can be debilitating, and have a detrimental effect on productivity.

Today, the UK has a sketchy reputation for productivity - certainly compared with countries like Germany, where process is respected and relied on for driving enviable efficiency and consistent high quality. Where the UK prides itself on its entrepreneurial, creative talent, Germany prides itself on getting the job done well, every time.

So there is a strong case for 'reimagining' process - for rebranding it as something positive, which can help to frame creativity and deliver something positive and repeatable from it, which can be continuously honed and improved over time - and embedded through structure.

What I mean is that, certainly here in the UK, we need to re-embrace process - not as a fixed and constraining force, but as a way of *harnessing* and *building on* our people's creativity. That way we get the best of both worlds.

We do actually do this in the world of science. The UK has been incredibly successful over the years and our scientists are incredibly creative people. Yet scientists don't randomly spin off in hundreds of different directions, creating things. They publish papers, pulling together knowledge, storing it and building on it over time. Science as an institution doesn't permit or promote chaos. Progress is collaborative and incremental: someone will come up with and test a theory, and someone else will build on it, or challenge it, and so leaps in discovery are made. The sense of shared ambition and purpose, and respect for discipline and rigour, that pervade science are quite awe-inspiring.

I believe there is room for the same kind of approach in business - whereby someone comes up with an inspired way of doing something and, rather than tearing it up, ignoring it and moving on, others refine and build on it with proposed tweaks and additions. Rather than reject an imposed process, leaders and managers would become more inclusive, inviting feedback so that good ideas are moulded into something really special that everyone supports.

The key to changing attitudes is to position process as the foundation on which everyone in an organisation can shape and improve the way that business operates.

Avoiding the downward spiral

The optimal process is one that is evolutionary and expansive, able to encompass successful embellishments or variants from what is documented, to create an even greater process. It is this positive cycle of continuous improvement that companies should strive for, rather than trying to stamp on individuals' creativity and drive them back to the rule book, resentful and demotivated.

People inherently aspire to self-mastery and a sense of purpose. Instinctively, they want more autonomy to work in the way that feels right and best. But if following their initiative puts them at odds with the process, and the rule-master, they can lose motivation and impetus. If they have their knuckles rapped and are pointed back to the rule book, they now find themselves mutely following a process they don't believe in or support. Disengaged and disempowered, they begin to work at half capacity, ceasing to give more than they have to because... "Well, what's the point?".

These once-motivated self-starters stop suggesting new ideas, seeing it as a battle to try to get improvements made because the process is too rigid and initiative is seen as unwelcome.

Sapped of their enthusiasm, some people will simply give up. At this point, you've essentially created an environment where no one bothers trying to offer value/go the extra mile, because it doesn't feel worth it – it won't be recognised or appreciated. The manager has achieved what he or she thought they wanted - compliance, but at what cost? Might it be a case of 'Be careful what you wish for?'

The manager may justifiably feel that they are the only one coming up with the good ideas now. Everyone else is just mechanically following the process, requiring micro management to elicit something exact, better or different. With rising distrust in their employees who are now either sticking rigidly to the rule book, or flouting the rules without caring, managers find themselves meddling in the business and causing new and bigger problems.

And so the situation spirals downwards. Before long, the business is in a poor state. The manager is working very hard but is disillusioned and unhappy. Everything is weighing heavily on their shoulders in terms of improving the way that things operate.

Reversing this scenario isn't easy, requiring a fresh leap of faith on both sides.

6

IMPACT ON CULTURE

Typically in organisations, many processes are managed badly or not at all. Activities that are core to the business tend to be automated or otherwise tightly controlled. In sales organisations, there will be defined sales processes. In a production company there will be prescribed methods of manufacturing. But in many businesses (even those that appear to be well run) most processes, especially the seemingly less critical ones, are not 'managed' at all.

Rather, the processes in place have evolved and taken on a life of their own. They go off in a particular direction, irrespective of any controls the management may have tried to put in place, so that over time any intended rigour is relaxed and subject to interpretation or embellishment. The business takes two steps forward and one step back, without a solid structure to impose an ideal method or guide desired behaviour.

We have discussed the cycle of demotivation, whereby enthusiasm is drained from self-starters who are discouraged from suggesting new or better ways of doing things and managers essentially become control freaks: hovering supervisors who don't trust their teams to do the job as well as they would. It's a lose-lose situation: before long, everyone dreads coming to work.

The sad truth is that managers allow these situations to arise rather than address the real underlying issues, such as:

- Why don't we have great processes?
- Why don't we have more control over the way people do things?
- Are we promoting an environment of creativity and empowerment?

Rather than addressing these higher issues, managers will become fixated on specific steps within specific processes, finding fault and reprimanding employees: "Don't do it like that!" Criticism which is highly demotivating, and a known trigger of occupational illness.

Let me share a brief anecdote to illustrate. I was talking to the chief executive of a company that's responsible for delivery of plumbing equipment to building sites. We met for lunch because he wanted to talk about implementing some of the methodologies that I've been discussing in blogs on my LinkedIn page.

He was complaining: "All my staff are stupid!"

I challenged this by asking, "What, all of them?!"

He had about 30 people in his business. It was a reasonable size, though it wasn't huge. But he was unhappy because he felt he was the only one going the extra mile. "These people just don't care," he said. "They want to simply turn up, do their job and go home."

I asked him to consider whether this blanket statement was actually true, or whether – if he really thought about it - he could pinpoint individuals that actually might care more, or be smarter, than he assumed.

He pondered this for a moment, then went away to give it some more thought. Ultimately, what I wanted to suggest to him was implementing a new methodology to run his business: specifically Gino Wickman's business model, the *Entrepreneurial Operating System* (EOS)[8] (Gino Wickman is the founder of EOS Worldwide, a leadership team development company). The model sets out six core business components - Vision, People, Data, Issues, Process and Traction – that companies need to define and align to be successful.

The CEO in question didn't yet have the components of a good team to enable him to put his business on the right road. My hunch was that, among his 30 people, there must have been four or five who could have formed a strong team around him, which would have helped him to run his business. But he was a long way from realising this.

Even when people were reporting to supervisors, the CEO would undermine these middle managers by speaking directly to individual staff if he felt an intervention was needed. He had been micro-managing his business for so long that he no longer had any confidence in his staff to function autonomously; in turn his staff felt so watched and distrusted that they gave the bare minimum.

I wanted to help him break this vicious cycle. There were several potential ways forward. The first was to create a culture of improvement in his business. But he wasn't there yet, so we took a step back and started

---

[8] EOS®, the Entrepreneurial Operating System, EOS Worldwide: https://www.eosworldwide.com/what-is-eos.

talking about building a team. Because the CEO felt that nobody was competent enough to form a team around him, he wanted to recruit from outside. He was looking to appoint a senior financial director to help him run the business, but this would have been a sidekick rather than a team - and an employee, rather than someone dedicated to working long hours and sharing his pain.

So his initial step, ironically, was to construct a team from within his staff. To do this, he needed to change himself first, and become less controlling so that employees would have the time and space to develop. This required a massive leap of faith on both sides, after such a negative spiral downwards. But, over time, his team did grow under him: they stopped being 'servants' and became equals who joined him in running the business.

From that point, it was much easier to move forward with other measures to instil greater accountability and a defined process. The CEO was then able to implement other components of the Entrepreneurial Operating System, and experienced a remarkable transformation of the way his business operated. It was a wonderful achievement.

Embracing flaws & failure

Another CEO was telling me how frustrated he was with his staff, saying, "It's incredible! One came to me this morning with a document for the process by which we install a security alarm system. But we already have a process I wrote years ago."

The employee had identified that mistakes were being made; that installations were not as good as they could be and things needed to be improved. He had also noticed that there seemed to be no documents to support the process, so he had used his initiative and created his own.

Rather than recognise the flaws and applaud the initiative, the CEO was irked that someone had questioned and redrawn a process he had set down two decades earlier. Yet the employee didn't know that such a document existed. This oversight, and the fact that he was berated for attempting to improve a situation, did not do much to boost the employee's morale. Having been reprimanded for his proactivity, he was unlikely to stick out his neck again in future for the benefit of the business.

It's not unreasonable that somebody at a more senior level might expect things to be done in an established and entrenched way. Yet, when a more junior member of staff views a situation with a fresh perspective and finds the courage to venture a suggestion, it can cause them significant despondency to find their idea ignored or even deliberately rejected.

No one is fundamentally at fault here: these reactions, on both sides, are simply human nature. So it is helpful to anticipate this kind of scenario and have some parameters in place for how to manage process and any proposed deviations from accepted practice: to ensure that initiative doesn't morph into rebellion; and that a desire for order and control doesn't mutate into dictatorship and an aversion to constructive feedback.

The ideal compromise is to create a robust framework: not a static document prescribing how things *must* be done, but rather 'living' best-practice guidelines - supported by a mechanism for communication, evolution and improvement. This mechanism then needs to be embedded in the business. It's hard to define what I mean by "embedded" but ultimately to me it means that the process isn't something disjoint from the activity like a file no one looks at but it is the activity and is what drives the activity. There are several ways to achieve this which we will cover later.

If I'm given a job to do at a junior level in a company and am not given full guidance on how to do it, I'm going to try to do my best but it's inevitable that this will not be perfect and that I will miss things. I'm going to have my own ideas and be inclined to pursue them because that's the only option open to me.

To avoid 'best guess' scenarios, staff need a structure and tools they can readily draw on, in the context of their role or immediate task - so they don't need to worry about forgetting things, or neglecting to attend to the smaller details that might seem less obviously important. Ideally this should be possible without staff having to proactively seek out the latest process documentation, wherever that might be. This will help new or temporary members of staff get up to speed quickly too.

Rather than being a one-way online instruction guide, however, this mechanism should allow employees to operate with autonomy, and provide constructive feedback about potential issues or scope for improvement to the current process.

Managers should be able to capture this creativity and consider, "Do we want to adopt these new ideas? How might we incorporate them into the bigger picture of how we work?". Far better this, than allowing employees to 'go rogue' each time the process feels at odds with the way they intuitively want to approach a task.

Building in scope for suggestions introduces the added, important bonus of making staff feel 'heard'. When their ideas are invited and considered (whether or not they go on to be accepted, rejected, partially included or contribute towards even better ideas), individuals feel listened to and valued, so will feel encouraged to come up with even better ideas in future. It's really that simple.

As I see it, most businesses are formed without proper foundations put in place to manage communication around how jobs are performed. Without any formal parameters in place to address these factors - which are critical in enabling employee empowerment, and for fostering creativity and feedback – companies will inevitably cultivate a culture of unhappiness.

7

POINTLESS DOCUMENTATION

We have identified that many businesses are inherently built on an unhealthy structure, which too often sees owners and managers seeking to reassert control as routine activities are carried out in haphazard, non-standard ways across the organisation, due to a lack of formal process.

A common response to this chaos is for managers to start to document processes – anxious to get rules down on paper. While this might seem to be a step in the right direction, towards improved consistency, it rarely solves the problem. More often than not, it's more of a security blanket for the owner/manager – a sense of taking back control, of having something formal to point people towards. When I've spoken to business leaders who have done this, they tend to say things like, "People move on. At least we know how things are being done," or "It's important to know how the business operates day to day." Commonly, they make reference to people being run over by buses...

But, in a vacuum, after-the-event process documentation achieves very little. When an employee does leave a business suddenly, it isn't actually the process that other people go to if they want to learn how to cover their role. Rather, they muddle through – already knowing roughly how to do things, even if not in the best possible way.

As an example, let's say I was working in a company and the finance clerk left, meaning that I've suddenly got to do the payroll. Even if there is a documented process in a file that tells me how to do the job, I would probably assume a gulf between the 'ideal' practice and what my former colleague did every day, and fall back on a combination of common sense and hazy recollection to determine what to do.

Which begs the question why managers bother documenting processes at all. If no one routinely consults them, why do business owners and managers expend so much time and energy setting down all their processes and putting them in a file? Even going to the trouble and expense of performing six-monthly or annual reviews, updating the documents to match current practice?

To me, it's a bit like tightening your belt to make yourself slimmer. It may make you feel better, but it doesn't alter the facts, you're fat and you need to lose weight. At best, it leads to something that can be used in training – albeit that the way people operate is usually different to what's written down, which essentially means that word-of-mouth will be the main means by which new people learn the ropes.

Having clearly documented processes in place might make your business more saleable; more attractive to a private equity firm or to a potential buyer. But even here process documentation is generally futile because it doesn't reflect the way your business actually operates, and potential investors will be wise to that.

Ultimately, process documentation without follow-through provides a false sense of security that a range of everyday business controls are in place, and that deviants from the process can be called to account.

But, given the misuse and abuse of such documents, it could be argued that process documentation for its own sake does more harm than good. I would certainly suggest that, unless strong process is embedded in the business and applied practically to day-to-day activity, with the feedback provision discussed earlier, they serve no real purpose at all.

The importance of embedding process

When I ran into quality and control problems with my own business, eShare - where I was meddling and I couldn't see a way to get the business working the way I wanted it to work - we identified the importance of *embedding process* in cementing recommended good practice into everyday activity.

In the last chapter, I explained the ramifications of having no process-based communication between manager and employee: the mismatch of expectations and reality. The manager has an expectation of how process should be done, and the employee behaves differently: there is a glaring disconnect. The only potential source of reconciliation is the document sitting in the file on the shelf (assuming there is one...).

To close the gap between expectation and reality, the documented process needs to be *embedded* in day-to-day business: that is, becoming something employees actually refer to as they do their job.

The origins of Process Bliss

The idea for my current business, Process Bliss, can be traced back to the billing procedure at eShare. The company was a young start-up. We didn't have any level of automation, and needed to send out an increasing number of invoices every month. When we had smaller numbers of clients, we would simply draft these and send them out: it was very easy. I would do it myself. But as we got to 10, 15, 20 customers who were signing up to our service, the invoicing process became increasingly difficult and time-consuming. And by now I needed to delegate the task.

This was not straightforward: the invoicing needed to be done in a certain way. I didn't see any point in documenting the process because no one would ever have consulted the file. Yet it was an impossible task for others to perfect without clear guidance, as so many nuances were involved. Eventually even I couldn't complete the task without making errors and forgetting steps. We found the answer was to devise a checklist for people to follow - using software, because we were a software company.

This was the origin of Process Bliss at eShare. As we developed our tool, the goal was simply to define how the job was done, so that when someone else performed the task each month they would know all the steps to follow. The wider potential was even more satisfying however, because the other thing we could do was attach the necessary documents for each everyday process.

So, rather than having countless, pointless documents gathering dust on the shelf—such as template invoices that we needed to send— we attached them to each monthly checklist so they could be edited and used. Essentially what we built was a Microsoft SharePoint site with a checklist and documents. We then added the ability to copy last month's site to create this month's. Each month we started with a billing site which not only gave us the checklist to follow so that we could tick off what we were doing but also all the documents from last month to update.

What's more if we wanted to amend our approach, rather than just do it differently and hope we remembered to do it again next month, we added extra steps to the checklist (or removed or edited them) and they would naturally carry forward to next month. We had a way of making change stick.

And because people began to realise that they weren't just doing it differently this month, they were making permanent change to our well thought through and regularly used process, they really started to consider whether the change was right. It stopped people destroying the process with ill thought through divergences.

It was powerfully transformative because anyone doing the job knew exactly what needed to be done, and had all the tools and notes they needed at hand but crucially they also had it within their power to improve the way it was done with the knowledge those improvements would stick.

So, while in essence we had documented the process, we had done this from the perspective of trying to *help* each person to do their job and empower them to do it better.

The airline industry, which we've already discussed with reference to emergency drills, is very good at taking this perspective on process – seeing it not so much as 'rules you must follow' but rather as a 'self-help aid'. Interestingly, if you look at the checklists provided for pilots, they're designed more than anything to *help* rather than *dictate to* the intended user. For example, great effort is taken to make sure they are not too long and to exclude steps the pilot will automatically adhere to.

In the book *Checklist Manifesto*[9], by Atul Gawande, a globally recognised surgeon, writer and public health leader, the author talks about a checklist for staff on a commercial aircraft discovering that a door has been left open after a plane has taken off. The process set out for the pilot involves managing the pressure in the cabin (important but not necessarily intuitive), yet not instructions to land at the nearest airport which the pilot would do instinctively if required. The point is to give the pilot instant help, without overloading him or her with excessive information.

Billing might not be quite in the same league as an airplane in distress, but again what will be of most value and most effective is making sure the individual has what they need to do the job as efficiently and accurately as possible. It shouldn't aim to cover every last detail, telling them things they would do naturally, but rather focus on providing support where it is likely to be needed most – where the best action might not be obvious or where the information might be hard to find.

[9] The Checklist Manifesto: How to Get Things Right, Atul Gawande, 2009.

Fundamentally though, what we are really doing is reversing a commonly accepted paradigm; "process is there to control people". Actually process is there to help people.

So I started to embed this approach, using the tool we had developed, into the eShare business, and it soon began to take on a life of its own - in that its potential quickly multiplied.

We realised we could start to assign steps to people, for instance. Then the software became a collaborative aid, pointing to the different things various people did: soon everyone had a keener understanding of where they fitted into the various processes.

They appreciated *why* they had to do certain things; they could see the part they played in the overall process. Better still, everyone instinctively wanted to use the tool, because it was easier than trying to remember how to do everything and it saved searching for the correct documents. It was a resounding success.

The key to this willing adoption lay in the *application* of the process guide. The content wasn't dissimilar to the documentation that was on the shelf, but the guidance was now *embedded within* the business. It was useful, in context, and readily available at the point of need. At this stage we had yet to implement a mechanism for feedback and for agreeing and controlling changes to the process, but we were clearly on the right track. We had created something that people embraced positively: a tool that helped rather than hindered them, and which didn't seek to curb their enthusiasm.

It was quickly becoming integral to the way people worked and part of the culture of the business, rather than something enforced from above that demands compliance, with no further discussion.

The next task was to give employees input into the process, as it continued to evolve. If you want to ***enhance*** the way process is done, or prevent employees from ***'going rogue'*** as new ideas occur to them, it's important to have a mechanism for process feedback and controlled improvements. So, along with a solid foundation for how things should be done, it's important to retain scope for people to hone and build on top of this, in a controlled manner.

When process is embedded into a business so that it helps people, it provides a base for progress. Because there is a structure in place, you can then ratchet this up. It is much less likely that employees will flout the process. If people want to amend and improve the process, fantastic! With the right controls in place, embedded within your business, all manner of positive progress is possible – keeping everyone engaged and moving towards the same goal: a better business experience for all.

You'll also be increasing accountability, once there is a tool that people are following and you can see that this is the case as employees tick off each step they complete. But again, it's worth leaving scope for employees to provide commentary within the tool, so that if they strongly feel a step isn't necessary or needs to be overridden in a particular case, they can explain why – providing the basis for a constructive discussion, which in turn provides an opportunity for process refinement and a better business.

Overcoming process's negative associations

When I first introduced 'process' at eShare, I didn't call it that. I knew 'process' was a dirty word. Instead, I referred to a new 'billing site' or 'recruitment site'. It just so happened that within these functional contexts, there would be relevant guidance and workflow to steer the way employees carried out tasks. Although this was 'process' at its strongest, I hesitated to refer to it in those terms because people have grown to have such negative associations with 'process' – for all of the reasons discussed in earlier chapters of this book. So often 'process' conjures up images of people being treated like robots - unthinkingly going through the motions, miserable and disengaged.

Without realising that a better-defined process was the goal, employees engaged with eShare's software tool, liked it and found it immensely helpful. Crucially they felt ownership of it, continuously thinking up other ways it could help them. Instead of seeing it as something controlling and monitoring them, they saw it as something empowering and in many ways liberating.

Reframed as 'a tool to help us all do a better job', 'process' at eShare became something welcome and desirable. By the time we eventually applied the word 'process', it was already accepted. We had successfully changed the culture.

Overcoming process resistance

When I first gave a presentation about Process Bliss - my current company, founded to take a formal version of the eShare tool to market – the network of CEOs in front of me were less than enthusiastic, they too having a tarnished perspective of 'process'. That's when I started referring to 'process' as "the dirty word".

"It kills creativity," one said. "I don't want people to be told to do this, and told to do that. I want them to think for themselves. As soon as you start introducing process to people, it just creates another pointless job for people to follow and they stop thinking."

Another echoed the point about removing people's initiative.

We've applied this feedback to our thinking about our product and how we market it, referring to Process Bliss predominantly as an empowerment tool that enables people to do a better job. But I'm not sure that people always believe it. As soon as they see the word 'process' they immediately think, "Yeah, right. But actually, what you're trying to do is take away my freedom and monitor me."

This resistance is a great shame, especially given the negative effects of chaos and a lack of structure. Without an agreed baseline, it is difficult to provide a pathway for process improvement. Too much is left to chance and interpretation, and great ideas have nowhere to be channelled resulting in mediocrity. Give people a clear starting point, and watch those opinions and ideas garner momentum.

The important point here is that it's not essential to nail the ideal process up front, but to set down some sensible parameters which can be built on over time – something that everyone might contribute to.

In the words of Tom Peters[10], a well-known American writer on business management practices, "Management is about arranging and telling. Leadership is about nurturing and enhancing." He also famously said, "Excellent firms don't believe in excellence – only in constant improvement and constant change."

So it makes sense that ambitious businesses would put in place structures for this: not rigid processes for employees to blindly follow, but rather tools to guide them as they hone best practice.

CEOs and business owners who have observed process done badly may understandably be sceptical about inviting employees to help craft and improve the way things are done. But if the mark of a good manager is their ability to make themselves largely redundant[11], then it follows that they need to equip their staff with the tools to do the best possible job – and instil in them a desire to keep improving.

---

[10] Tom Peters, author of *In search of excellence: Lessons from America's best-run companies*: https://tompeters.com/.

[11] Make Yourself Redundant: Why All Effective Leaders Enjoy Vacation, Leadership strategy article,
Louis Efron, *Forbes*, August 29, 2013:
https://www.forbes.com/sites/louisefron/2013/08/29/make-yourself-redundant-why-all-effective-leaders-enjoy-vacation/.

Unfortunately, many leaders arrive in the role without formal training. They have risen through the ranks or pursued a new business idea without anyone preparing them to spearhead a company or lead a team. Too often they dictate rather than empower, and see process as an extension of that desire for control. They don't fully understand the concept of empowerment, and that what most people want out of work is a level of autonomy and a chance to make a difference.

But what if the right tools could turn that situation around?

8

THE SOLUTION

We've spent some time looking at why process is crucial to business success, for example in ensuring a consistent service and providing the parameters for continuous improvement. We've also considered why it's so hard to implement good process, and what's behind the temptations for people to go their own way.

Whatever the preconceptions about process, most people appreciate it when a business is organised, consistently delivers a great service, looks after its customers in a reliable way, and communicates well internally. The parts they like less are when they feel forced to jump through hoops for what seems like no good reason, and/or when people feel they are being closely watched out of a lack of trust.

So the key to progress must be to reconcile everyone with a process that makes sense to and works for everyone. One which isn't over-egged, but is just right for those who need it.

A great place to start, then, is to determine the optimal level of detail needed to support those in a particular role to do their job to the best of their ability – constructed in a way that is useful, practical and non-distracting.

A less-is-more principle works well when putting together checklist processes, on the basis that "When everything is important, nothing is important" – that is, if a process is basically a comprehensively detailed description of 100 things to do, people will ignore it. But if it's a checklist of a few critical things that people might forget in the heat of the moment, employees will embrace it as an indispensable aid. In fact it can help to highlight particularly critical items on the checklist, as a visual cue for times of pressure.

"When everything is important, nothing is important."

There is a secondary purpose to the checklist, of course - other than supporting the person doing the job. This is to reassure line managers or business owners that crucial steps have been completed. But business leaders /managers need to treat this facility with caution, and try to resist using it to control or catch out staff.

Another friend of mine is CEO of a professional services business. She picked on a rather trivial aspect of the company's recruitment process, insisting that she wanted to see reports showing that the particular step had been performed: specifically that an email is circulated to the team when someone new joins the business. Clearly, communication is important. But did the CEO really need a report to be reassured that this was happening? If the recruitment process was fit for purpose and clearly set out, she ought to have been able to trust that such tasks were being completed routinely.

It emerged that she had been burnt in the past when this step had been skipped. So now she had been drawn into micro-management, something she had hoped to avoid. And all over something that hardly jeopardised the finances of the business or some aspect of compliance. Yes, the task should be carried out, but should it fall to the CEO to monitor for omission?

Checklists get round this issue. Just as cleaners still walk the corridors of many hotels with checklists on their trolleys, and nurses check off patient routines on boards above or at the end of hospital beds, having a clear marker of activities lets everyone see that tasks have been done or where along a process people have got to. It's an aide-memoire to the 'doer', while offering clarity or reassurance to colleagues and supervisors. It needn't be threatening.

As I'll come onto later in this book, if they're asked to tick boxes people will generally oblige. If a tick is missing, then, it is a fairly reliable mechanism to capture when something has *not* been done. Simple, yet effective. Certainly far better in the moment than having to send an email or file a report – the kind of protracted activity that people put off, avoid or become annoyed by.

An electronic tick-box makes all of this even more convenient and easy to manage. It is a really simple way to capture data and to make sure that this is communicated (whether on a proactive or reactive basis) to everyone involved in the business.

Although not everyone responds warmly to box-ticking, presenting this in the right way should overcome most barriers. When we talk to people about how to implement checklists, they often instinctively try to put in place excessive controls which can make processes unworkable. These controls fall into three categories:

- Forced steps
- Forced sequence
- Forced assignment

These controls need to be thought through carefully as they can not only make the processes unworkable but they also form the basis of why people often hate process. Fortunately, it's fairly easy to get past these concerns.

Forced steps

Often a primary intention with a process is to create a structure that ensures that pivotal steps cannot be carelessly skipped, knowingly sidestepped or blatantly ignored. A forced step is something that *has* to be done. And generally speaking, if something is that important and it says so on the checklist, it will be done. Unless, for some reason, a person *isn't* able to do it. But what then? What happens to the process, and to its onward evolution?

When someone hits a practical barrier with a process, this could provide valuable business information – as long as there is some kind of mechanism to capture what has happened, so that these insights can be fed into process refinement or service improvements.

Take the process of 'onboarding' a customer. I may decide that filing a signed contract will form an essential step, before anything else can progress, for instance.

However, what happens if things deviate from the plan? The customer may ask to pay in cash up front, or to put down a deposit, for example – thus potentially obviating the need for a contract, in the case of our software. Or there may be some other reason why they can't sign or don't wish to sign a contract, yet they are still a desirable customer whose business we don't want to turn away.

So what's the answer, if the process demands acknowledgement of a completed contract before next steps can progress? A 'yes/no' checklist response doesn't allow for less black-and-white situations. What's really needed is an option to explain when and why a step has not been completed. Information which can then be fed back to the business; and into process refinement.

That is, we need to build an understanding of the particular circumstances - giving the business the ability to consider what should happen in other similar scenarios. Perhaps new contingency plans will involve terms and conditions around a customer deposit; or perhaps there will need to be an alternative plan to ensure that any part-payment is sufficient to cover the costs of the project.

And so we begin to re-examine our procedures; perhaps amend them and improve our whole business. But we can only do that if we have feedback mechanisms.

Such mechanisms are welcomed by employees too, because they're able to explain their thinking if ever they feel they have no choice but to diverge from the steps set out for them.

Forced sequence

Similarly, there will be times when circumstances will prevail, which mess with the logical order in which steps are supposed to be completed. And if the process is so rigid that it does not allow for this, grinds to a halt or incurs delays because of it, or has to be abandoned altogether once a step has been missed, then it may not be fit for purpose.

So, while there will always be an optimum way of doing things, and logical progression of steps to achieve this, again the process needs to leave room for exceptions and associated explanations.

Take the case of invoice payment. Ordinarily, a business would specify that this can't happen until the invoice has been officially approved and signed off for payment - an essential, non-negotiable, sequential step in the process. Yet there may be circumstances where it's not possible to get approval within the timeframe needed, when it's critical that the invoice is paid. Perhaps the approver is unavailable or uncontactable.

The processor may need to take a judgement call and override the system, making an exception in which approval is sought retrospectively, after the event. But, for the sake of business control and due diligence, it's important that bypassing controls does not happen routinely and that there is scope to record when and why this happens, and the sequence of steps taken in these exceptional cases.

By capturing this valuable business information, a company can start to determine alternative courses of action, to avoid similar scenarios in future. The business might deduce that it shouldn't be relying on a single individual to approve invoices, and grow the team, for instance. Or it might determine that a change in the authorisation limit is appropriate – because closer inspection reveals that the processor's justification for paying certain invoices without official approval was that those payments' were relatively low value.

What soon becomes clear is that process flexibility and transparency can *improve* process rigour, by ensuring that the steps set out fit the purpose and are a help rather than a hindrance to the work people do.

Forced assignment

Being too specific about who must or can complete a particular task can also create stumbling blocks, in certain situations, so here too it is important that businesses consider scope for exceptions management. The intentions behind 'forced assignment' – *ie* that a step can only be completed by a certain individual – are generally wise and well thought-through. But again there is a risk that excessive rigidity can hamper progress and/or prompt abandonment of prescribed steps.

That's because imposing rigid rules can render systems unworkable or bring them to a halt when the exact conditions cannot be met – for instance, if the nominated individual is off sick, tied up in back-to-back meetings, or on leave.

If teams are able to find temporary workarounds, the risk is that (a) auditable information about this is not recorded, and (b) that staff 'go rogue' or down tools.

If assigning a particular individual, or someone with a specific rank, is deemed essential for a particular task, then it's important to consider what could, might and should happen in scenarios when these conditions cannot be met, or at least provide the means for staff to capture details about times they are forced to think laterally and deviate from the script.

If a task is indeed completed by another person, information about the issues, decisions and outcomes will allow managers to analyse these scenarios and determine whether they indicate a problem in your business that may need to be addressed. For example, should more people be trained and authorised to complete that task, to avoid the risk of unqualified team members doing an inadequate job?

In later chapters, we will set out some guiding principles to help you overcome some of these challenges which can make it tricky to implement processes and supporting technology.

Mind-set

We've looked at the need to strike the right balance of process detail, without forcing staff through unnecessary hoops or inadvertently de-emphasising the important steps amid overly-detailed task descriptions. Process also needs to be something that people enjoy.

Almost every business owner who tries to implement any sort of process usually designs and imposes it from above, with the aim of bringing staff into line so that they consistently comply with what's required. It is not typically an inclusive exercise, initiated from the perspective of employees, to empower them to do their jobs confidently and well.

Too often process, and making sure everyone complies with it, is seen as the owner/manager's responsibility. Although this seems logical, it would be much better for everyone if creating, refining and updating process was a shared endeavour. Something that everyone saw value in, and embraced accordingly. Where process is seen as something that empowers people to shine in their roles, business managers are able to create a more positive mind-set around it – as something everyone jointly owns and has a say in. In turn, equipped with the right tools to support them in their jobs, employees are likely to find greater satisfaction in - and give more to - their work.

Clarity & communication

Among the most critical determinants of process success are clarity and communication, which is where technology can help. Instead of people checking up on each other and issuing instructions and reminders to keep everyone on track, software ensures that simple, timely prompts are issued automatically as workflow progresses through the system.

So process isn't only a tool to support employees; supported by software, it also closes the loop on communication as tasks are automatically handed on from one team member to the next. No more risk of next steps being overlooked or forgotten, no need for 'nagging' reminders, and no more finger-pointing. Everyone simply does their part, checks it off the progress list and moves on.

The other wonderful by-product of a software-supported process is its tracking facility. If the goal is to empower staff to do their best work, freely and without overbearing supervision, then an inherent audit trail provides the comfort factor for both managers and employees.

This enables owner/managers to keep track of what's going on and pinpoint any recurring issues so that interventions or improvements can be targeted if and when needed. Employees, meanwhile, have the reassurance that all of their efforts are being registered in real time as they go about their tasks, providing a definitive and impartial record of their conscientiousness.

In my old business eShare, we would develop a new product feature and then tell the sales team to sell it, the marketing team to let clients know about it and the support team to look after customers struggling with it. That sounds perfectly sensible. The issue was one of timing.

The sales and support teams would need 1 month's notice to prepare the relevant training and the marketing team would need 2 months notice to perform adequate communication with clients about the forthcoming features.

Failure to meet these timescales lead to unhappy customers who rather than eagerly looking forward to the new features that they knew were coming, were angry about the disruption caused by the system changes we made without any build up communication. This was exacerbated by a support team that when asked how the new features worked, weren't sure.

We had managed to turn the great new features that we had invested in to make our customers' lives so much better into something that they didn't want, didn't appreciate and made them more likely to leave.

Our inability to communicate between departments meant that we weren't performing the activities we needed to at the right time.

To give an analogy if three of us were cooking a Sunday roast. It was like one person cooking the meat and then only once the meat was ready did they tell the other people to cook the roast potatoes and the vegetables.

It sounds extreme but this is how many businesses operate and communicate.

The solution wasn't rocket science, once we had implemented process properly, we had time and system driven notifications that ensured that at early stages in the development process the relevant processes within the sales, support and marketing departments were triggered.

9

PROCESS IS FOR EMPLOYEES

When I set up Process Bliss, I hired my former executive assistant at eShare to come and work with us. Laura was mad about process, and fully supported the software we had created and the new business I'd set up around it. She appreciated the potential for instilling a certain order in a business, without stifling people's creativity.

One day we decided to recruit a new marketing assistant, and immediately Laura went off to set the wheels in motion according to how she felt it should happen, and in fact how we had approached the recruitment process at eShare.

Yet I'd revised my views on this, and felt very much that our new approach should be to identify the best candidates based on talent over and above experience. The process I'd devised was by no means perfect, little more than the bare bones to solving the recruitment issue. This boiled down to ignoring CVs initially, in favour of personality and aptitude testing. But it was important to me that we built on that process.

When I realised that Laura had defaulted to her own way of working, rather than adopting my new work-in-progress, we sat down to review the situation and eventually merged the two approaches to create an exceptional process.

The bigger issue, though, was that she'd instinctively ignored the new process, ploughing on with established practice which she felt had served the need well up to now.

It caused me to pause and think. How, as owner/managers, do we ensure that people follow a desired process?

I believe the key is ensuring that the process is something quite indispensable – that is, something that's relevant and of value to the people who will follow it. If they see the sense in it, and it genuinely helps them to get their best results, then why wouldn't they buy into it? If, on the other hand, it makes their working life harder and appears to hamper their creativity and productivity, a response of resistance or anarchy is similarly understandable.

At eShare, the hardest teams to bring into line were the sales people, who prided themselves on their instinct, worked largely from gut-feel and memory, and generally did everything differently each time. This was a sensitive situation to address. The last thing the business wanted was to upset the creative flow and success rate of our sales people, but at the same time we needed to ensure consistency to the customer experience as they came on board and started to use our products. As the sales people were usually the first contact clients had with the company, they set the tone for everything that followed. So it was important to get that right.

We addressed this by ensuring that the sales people gained something from following the desired process; that it intrinsically supported desirable outcomes for them. The customer on-boarding process was the simplest way for them to generate a contract without any errors. It also became the means by which they most quickly received their commission. That is, we made the customer on-boarding process something sales people would want to get right, first time, every time. In this way, we ensured that sales contracts were completed and stored systematically, and so on.

At the same time, we also made sure not to eke out the customer on-boarding process so that it became something cumbersome and irritating to the sales team. Wherever possible, we passed less critical parts/ancillary administration tasks to other people in the business. The sales team appreciated being relieved of the 'paperwork', while the business benefited from making better use of its most expensive assets - the sales team, who could now spend more time doing what they were paid for.

Enforcing process improvements isn't always that straightforward, however. Sometimes, it requires more of a cultural shift to encourage new kinds of behaviour.

Fostering a culture of collaboration

At my current company, Process Bliss, I was very keen to replicate a joined-up/collaborative software release procedure we had introduced at eShare, enabled by proactive communication across the business about forthcoming product releases or updates. Once bedded in, the process worked very well.

The basis of the process was that a product development department doesn't, or shouldn't, operate in isolation. Kicking off the software release process would trigger other departments to start their planning at an early stage. For instance, it would assign tasks to the marketing department who could start to drive market momentum by promoting what was to come. In the meantime, the sales team were made aware that a new release was coming and about any special features and functionality so that they could formulate their pitches.

Support were kept in the loop, too, so they would be ready to advise and help customers with the new release once live; and Finance so they could factor any changes into billing.

Too often, product development teams neglect these wider elements, seeing their task as simply to bring a revised or new product to market.

It took a while to ingrain the new behaviour. We implemented the process, but after a while people reverted to doing their own thing again. Once the process was underway it worked beautifully but the product development team simply failed to start it, and operated from memory – with the result that problems started to occur as people weren't informed.

The key to permanently resetting people's mind-set came when the product development team finally understood the havoc that is created when the rest of the business wasn't aware of or aligned with new product releases until the last minute. Suddenly the penny dropped, they could see the consequences of not using the process reverberate through the business, and they realised how important it was to use the process we had in place.

In the meantime, to lower resistance to the new process, we revised the steps involved so that every task was justified and of value, and there were no extraneous hoops for busy teams to jump through. Once the new system worked for everyone, it took off.

Selling the vision

The point is that people need to be taken on a journey towards good process, understanding why it's being brought in, who it's for and how they personally will benefit from it. Once everyone understands the bigger picture, resistance should give way to acceptance, ownership and enthusiastic adoption.

For the owner-manager, the realisation is about the importance of viewing and treating process not as a management tool, but rather as a supportive tool for staff: one that does more than dictate what to do; and guides the user towards the best possible result in the most efficient and effective way.

So if they are performing an annual task, such as filing accounts, which feels fairly onerous and daunting and requires data to be pulled together from multiple sources, the process and supporting software points them to the data from last year along with other useful prompts and pointers to complete the task efficiently and accurately this year. From employee appraisals and customer review processes, to regulatory reporting, an optimised process guided by an automated tool, should replace uncertainty, stress and pressure with clarity and confidence through targeted help.

What is it that the target users might need to know to complete a task? Why not include the facility to be able to add other information, so that if they find there's something that the process doesn't help them with they can add it in for future reference. That way, you'll be ensuring that the next person has that additional information too. Include links to relevant documents, resources and contact details in your process support tool - whatever might be needed to help people complete the particular process as efficiently as possible.

Once the mechanism becomes indispensable in this way, people will use it by default.

Adapting to the way people learn

We need computers to perform complex calculations. Similarly, we need tools to help us to remember all the steps in a process. If I ask my members of staff to memorise the mathematical constant of *pi* (π) to 50 places, it's not unreasonable to imagine that they would struggle or fail. But I could quite easily give them some way of recording the answer and reading it back to me.

It seems astonishing in this day and age that, when we have such great technology, owner/managers allow people to fail - and then criticise them for doing so, when really it's down to us for not supplying the supportive tools that would help them succeed. We create complex tasks which we expect people to remember and execute flawlessly, and wonder why everyone is stressed and miserable at work.

Educational systems need to keep up with the times, reducing the emphasis on forcing people to learn and remember facts by rote - as though they wouldn't have access to tools and resources to look things up at some later date. In the digital era, I would argue that it's more important we know *where to find knowledge*, rather than trying to retain an encyclopaedia worth of facts in our brains. Today, if you want to diagnose a medical condition, repair a car, or cook a recipe, you no longer need a photographic memory. That information is readily accessible and easily searchable online. Having the skills to distil, scrutinise and apply knowledge is a far more useful skill.

The same ought to be true at work. Instead of expecting people to learn a process, and then admonishing them when they get it wrong, wouldn't it be better to empower them and make them instantly self-sufficient, by pointing them to the aids that will support them on getting things right first time, every time? If we can stop trying to drum excessive process information into people's brains, we might free up their time and energy for being creative and adding value.

Indeed, this has been my own experience as I have learnt to release the reins and entrust process to the people in my business, so that I no longer have to try to control everything, making everyone stressed and miserable! It took a leap of faith to hand over to them. But I knew that I was going to be able to see whether things were being followed, and I was looking forward to having the kind of business that runs itself.

Before long, despite having the opportunity to check what was being done and get that reassurance, I found I no longer needed or wanted to look. I knew I had provided the tools to empower my staff to do a really great job. If they deviated from the process as set out, I knew it would be for reasons that they had thought through, and that I, or they, would be able to analyse those scenarios more closely if appropriate.

The positive impact on everyone's happiness, and on my relationship with my team, was considerable. I experienced a huge growth in trust in my staff and I began to have more time to be creative in the business myself. Once my employees were empowered, they started suggesting improvements to the way we did things. The kind of oversight and control that I thought that I wanted disappeared. It was a powerfully liberating experience. From that point, transformation happened quite quickly. People relaxed, and became more creative. If they had a great idea, they could attempt to see it through and make a difference in the business.

I realised that, until I had changed the way I thought about and tried to manage process, my company had suffered a huge lost opportunity - that is, my ability to stand back and see the bigger picture for the business, and have the time and inclination to develop it.

"The less I do, the better it gets."

After turning that situation around, I found myself commenting to my EA on more than one occasion, "It's wonderful: the less I do, the better it gets."

10

PEOPLE ARE SMARTER THAN PROCESS

At the beginning of this book, I recalled an experience which undermined years of customer loyalty shown by my family to a hotel group. When rigid, ingrained process determined that they could not and would not refund us for a forced cancellation, just slightly beyond the window specified, we were made to feel that our long-standing customer relationship, and the large financial value we had represented to them, counted for nothing. We asked for a little flexibility, but the system did not allow for it, and even the management could not or would not overrule it.

I'll share a bit more here about the scenario as it unfolded, as to this day I find it disappointing, upsetting and unfathomable from a commercial/customer service/customer retention perspective. It is a lesson that other businesses ignore at their peril!

If you've even been camping with small children and you really want them to go to sleep, but they don't want to, there's not much you can do about it. And it can make for the most unpleasant of evenings - especially if you're on holiday, and even more so if you are in a small tent.

We wanted desperately to sleep but our two-year old, presumably excited by the adventure, wanted to stay up all night crawling around all over us. This is what we happened to be doing one summer night in the New Forest.

The refusal-to-sleep situation had been playing out night after night, until, when we were all finally sleeping peacefully, our tent was attacked by horses. Soon afterwards, cattle were mooing, and, suffice to say, by the next morning we felt shattered. We couldn't face another night like it, but didn't want to cut short the holiday.

We drove along a road, and before long a sign led us to a lovely manor house with fantastic gardens. It turned out to be a hotel. It had a room for us, and we had the most amazing experience – the hotel, the restaurant, and being rescued from our camping nightmare. We had such an enjoyable experience that we returned many times over the next few years, becoming familiar faces. Each time, the staff would welcome us by name and we would find a handwritten note in our room welcoming us back. Anyone who runs a hotel will know that this kind of experience takes a well thought-out process.

It turned out there were several hotels in the group, which was growing steadily. Over time we stayed at all of them - several times, particularly the original one. We even booked our week-long Summer vacations there for several years running , with our family of 6 taking up three double rooms and eating in their restaurants most lunchtimes and dinners. That was until we had to suddenly cancel a stay at a hotel on the south coast, and tried to activate the 72-hour cancellation policy - unfortunately with just 71 hours to go until our stay.

And this was when all those years of symbiotic relationship and goodwill were tested to breaking point. The person on reception said we couldn't cancel. We explained our circumstances, and that we had stayed with the hotel quite a lot, and in fact were only an hour over the cancellation threshold, still leaving them three days to re-book the room. We asked if they might talk to the manager, which they did but the answer was the same: sorry, but no. We were advised that we could try to take up the matter with the booking company: we tried three times. No one called us back.

Suddenly, our experience was becoming dire, and our feelings towards the hotel group soured. In a single scenario, they had undermined everything that had gone before, making us resentful that they couldn't be flexible when I had probably spent in the region of £15,000 with them over the years.

Still now, recalling the experience brings up the feelings we were left with: that our custom didn't matter after all; that keeping to the rules, and sticking to the process was all that counted.

So what went wrong? Clearly, a lot had been right with the hotel group's process as our consistently good previous experiences had borne out. People followed the process, and it was embedded in the business. Yet when it came to an exceptional situation, the manager and staff did not have the freedom to adapt the process, in the interests of maintaining the loyalty of a valued customer. Instead, they were controlled by it. There was no 'override' facility, no allowance for the people executing the process to exercise discretion. The process was so tightly structured that it failed the business at a crucial point. In insisting on the 72-hour cancellation policy, it risked curtailing thousands of pounds of repeat business. Not to mention negative reviews, and the warnings we would be issuing to friends and family as the result of our experience.

The lesson here is that when process controls people to the point that they cannot think for themselves, and apply intelligence and discretion when exceptional circumstances call for it, it risks damaging the business.

So it isn't sufficient to create a process that supports staff in doing their best work; there also needs to be a recognition that *process is not as important as the people who execute it.*

Ultimately, people are superior to and smarter than process and if they feel their hands are tied and they are being forced through steps that don't make sense or feel right, there will be a backlash somewhere along the line.

If someone doesn't want to do a step, or if they consider it stupid, they won't do it - even if the checklist is staring back at them. Attempting to control people through process is a very bad idea.

"If people feel their hands are tied and they are being forced through steps that don't make sense or feel right, there will be a backlash somewhere along the line."

Managing exceptions

One of our clients runs a software company, and he was implementing a process for the distribution of key fobs, to allow people access to certain parts of his building. He wanted to ensure people couldn't be issued with a key fob unless they met certain requirements and they had passed certain checks.

On the face of it, this made sense. Yet when I probed further, asking what would happen if someone turned up to a role without having had those checks, it turned out key fobs would typically be issued anyway and checks performed later, to avoid queues building up in the hallways.

Software wouldn't necessarily solve this issue, either. If the rule is that key fobs cannot be issued until checks have been performed, this could force staff to falsely declare that checks have been done. Or they may not even record that key fobs have been issued, because they're unable to tick the box around checks being performed.

Ultimately, trying to control people with process is impossible. A more practical approach, then, is to capture where process falls down, and where these breaches of protocol are occurring, so that you are aware of these issues. This awareness gives you an opportunity to improve your business – in this case, by deciding whether it's actually necessary to perform those checks before issuing key fobs, or ensuring that new employees are given plenty of warning before they arrive at the office that the checks will need to be performed.

Again, this is about applying process to empower and guide people, rather than control them and restrict their ability to apply reason and common sense in a situation.

Trying to control people through process won't work anyway, and people are always smarter than process so it's more important to give them freedom to diverge from a specified instruction and capture information about why this was necessary and what was done differently, to fit the exceptional scenario. A smart employee will usually go off-script anyway when a situation calls for it – unless it's absolutely essential that they don't. So why not build in a capability to record and learn from those situations?

Closing the loop: cultivating continuous improvement

If we are going to create a business where there's a culture of continuous improvement, then we need to facilitate people being able to do things in a different way, too. They need to be able to try things out, to learn whether something works or doesn't, and to adapt the process accordingly. If we try to control with process, we kill that kind of creativity.

The highly esteemed book by Matthew Syed, *Black Box Thinking*[12], talks about the importance of a closed-loop for ensuring that people and businesses learn from and make improvements based on their mistakes. The reference to a black box makes the parallel with the airline industry, where black boxes are included as standard in aircraft, to capture detail across the duration of a flight so that, in the event of an incident, it is

[12] Black Box Thinking: Why Some People Never Learn from Their Mistakes - But Some Do, Matthew Syed, 2015: https://www.goodreads.com/book/show/24611735-black-box-thinking.

possible to trace back precisely and determine what happened, what was done, and what went wrong.

This feedback isn't used solely for immediate investigative purposes, but also for feeding back into aircraft design and safety procedures, so that problems that can be designed out are not knowingly repeated. It is why flying is such a safe way to travel.

But in so many circumstances across other industries, the feedback loop is unstructured, inconsistent or non-existent, with the result that mistakes continue to be made and opportunities for improvement are missed. Unfortunately, we sometimes see this in healthcare, where great pressure on services can mean that follow-up processes are not always completed.

My father-in-law suffered a series of mini-strokes some months before his death at the age of 65. It was clear to his family that this had happened – we had seen TV awareness campaigns about the symptoms, and knew the importance of acting quickly - and we took him to see the GP on several occasions. He was scheduled for a hospital scan, but told that there was no great emergency: the GP was not convinced that he had had a stroke. While we were waiting for the scan, my father-in-law had a stroke that killed him. We felt that this was because the health service had not responded quickly enough.

We wondered what would happen in response to this: would anything be changed to ensure our experience was not repeated? Would there be airline-like vigilance in examining what went wrong, with the findings fed directly into safety enhancements? The answer was nothing. Nobody learned anything. Quite the contrary, everybody wanted to brush the mistake under the carpet and move on.

Of course no organisation, no team, no individual likes to own up to oversights, mistakes, inadequate practice. But wouldn't it be so much better for everyone if we could promote a culture where it's okay to admit that something went wrong? That perhaps something could be tweaked, tightened or completely transformed in a process to ensure those same errors or omissions are not repeated? Failing, learning, and continuously adapting and changing processes is the only real way to ensure improvement and better outcomes over time. Ignoring problems won't make them go away.

And the benefits of learning from and acting on failure and feedback could be multiple, depending on the context. For instance, the customer experience is likely to improve/employees will be happier and more confident/products or services will be safer and more efficient to deliver/ finances will be healthier/ business debts will be collected on time.

Collating feedback/incident logs/process deviations in a central database is a good idea, so that a record is built up which can be referred back to, and used for analysis and reports – for distilling trends that can help direct attention to where improvements may be needed most. If this knowledge can be shared readily, so much the better for those with an interest in process innovation and improvement.

In the UK, the Air Accident Investigation Bureau publishes reports which explore how air accidents have occurred, particularly those involving serious injury or death. I am a pilot myself, so I read these reports to improve my own technique because flying a plane does involve risks. So it's important that the people who operate planes understand and avoid the mistakes others have made.

Even if you have attempted to capture this kind of feedback in your own business, if you are not recording it systematically in a central place, sharing the findings and learning from your mistakes, then consider what value it really has. Are you merely collating evidence for auditors, or to cover yourself in the event of an insurance claim, or are you being proactive and positive in the way you apply this knowledge, to keep improving what you do?

The value of mistakes

In performance charts, managers often view 'red' areas as evidence of poor or failed delivery, but this is short-sighted. When it comes to monitoring process, red simply tells you that steps either haven't been performed correctly, or haven't been performed at all. The important question to delve into is why.

If we're running a recruitment campaign in our business, and one step as part of this process is to advertise the role on our web pages, if that step has not been performed it could be that there is a problem with the web site. We shouldn't automatically assume that someone has wilfully bypassed an important part of the recruitment process.

If outstanding customer payments are supposed to be chased fortnightly, but this hasn't happened in a particular case, this could be a sign of a deeper issue. On seeking to understand what has gone wrong once alerted, we might discover that a customer is unhappy and that, as a result, everyone feels uncomfortable chasing the unpaid invoice. Once this has become clear, we can take an alternative approach to resolve the issue and collect the money.

Exceptional behaviour and divergence from process can provide valuable clues about how to do business better, so think twice before castigating people for deviating from process and following their own path as there may well be a good reason.

11

PEOPLE WANT TO MAKE A DIFFERENCE

Once it has been established in the minds of both management and the wider business that process exists and is designed to support people to do their jobs confidently and well, the next step should be to hand over the ownership and control of the process, partially or wholly, to the team who will apply it. They should be the ones to hone and develop it over time, and be responsible for making it as good as possible.

I have learnt the value of this in my own businesses: not just the relief of being able to let go, but also the power of putting process in the hands of the people who will drive it. Once I let go of the controls, it became a question of how to encourage and harness people's creativity - not just in giving them the freedom to deviate from the script if ever they needed to, but also in allowing them an influence over the process itself and how it's developed and changed over time.

This isn't a new idea. The architects of business process reengineering, Michael Hammer and James Champy, wrote a book about process reengineering back in the 1980s[13], noting that for organisations to operate in the most efficient manner possible, they must give control of process

[13] Reengineering the Corporation: A Manifesto for Business Revolution, by Michael Hammer, James Champy, HarperCollins: https://www.harpercollins.com/9780060559533/reengineering-the-corporation/.

to the people involved. One priority must be to listen to what they are saying, and to do this continuously.

Harnessing process frustration

One means of showing staff their viewpoints are valued is to monitor and capture details of any deviation from process, as we've already discussed. And, rather than come down heavily on individuals for wandering away from the rules, it is a good idea to review and discuss the scenario, or at least commend the team member concerned for thinking outside of the box when an exceptional scenario presented itself.

Another approach is to capture real-time feedback on a process *while* people are operating it. So, at every stage of the process, there is a means for employees to add a note or insert a question. This provides an opportunity for people to prompt for more information that would help them progress a task more confidently or efficiently, or suggest improvements (different steps, improvements to existing steps, or whatever). By capturing feedback on the fly, you can be confident of not missing anything (which might be forgotten later), and of releasing pressure from team members at potential points of stress, by providing a practical outlet.

Then, the important thing is to make sure that all of this feedback is collated, analysed and acted upon. (If teams feel their feedback is being put aside or ignored, they will soon lose the motivation to provide it.) Once the team can see that their feedback has been absorbed into the process, they will be inspired to continue offering suggestions, to the benefit of the whole business.

It is a good idea to spell this out, so that employees feel their efforts are valued and having an impact. One obvious way of doing this is to sit down with all those that have provided feedback, or adapted what they do from the original process, and include them in conversations about designing and making specific improvements. Full, 360-degree feedback encourages individuals to keep providing feedback and ideas, and to assume ownership for addressing frustrations in the business.

This can be highly motivating, and quickly defuse tension or resentment that can build when people think their opinions don't matter, and that they have no influence over what they do - or how they feel - at work. (Too often in a business, there are people who complain about the way things are run but who feel powerless to change anything.) The goal should be to create an inclusive culture, ultimately going on to hire people who thrive in this kind of environment – where initiative is applauded and actively encouraged.

When I transformed the business culture at eShare, I found that after years of feeling that I was the only one who cared and had ideas, I now had 70 people primed and ready to help build a better business. Engagement levels soared, and attrition rates dropped - people liked working there, and stayed.

So the benefits of giving people ownership of process could be multiple. You might reduce your recruitment costs and retain more talent, finding that the really good people stay (in many businesses it's often the most creative people with the best ideas who leave, if they feel their potential isn't being harnessed and they have no scope to demonstrate their talent). Moreover the business will be able to tap into greater, collective brainpower, accelerating its improvement and innovation cycle – without the need to engage expensive consultants. The insights will be far more valuable too, because they're coming from the people who are actually doing the job, and encountering the issues or spotting the missed opportunities in your business - day in, day out.

It is through these opportunities that we have a chance to make a business special. In our own case, as a result of good process, which staff have helped to refine, we can have confidence that when someone arrives on their first day of work everything will be in place to give them a positive, memorable experience. Not just the practical things like an email account, but also something personal to welcome them – such as the new-starter's favourite snacks, or something else we've discovered about them during the hiring process.

These small touches set the tone by making the individual feel welcome and a part of things, building their trust and helping the team to gel. We make sure we do these things well, because we know it is important. The message we want to transmit to people joining our company, is that they don't just work for any old employer, but for one that pays attention and takes care of the details. If we want people to make a difference, we must show that we value them, recognise them as individuals, and will support them so that they can shine. This sounds easy but if you don't have some form of collaborative checklist onboarding process to all follow, it will slowly die and you will spend hours of wasted time trying to revive it, and ultimately you will almost certainly give up.

If they feel ownership of their role and how they do their job, your people will want to make a difference for customers too – because this is how businesses succeed and grow, and because it feels good to meet and exceed customers' expectations. An added dimension to this in the 21st century is that exceptional customer experiences (good or bad) can quickly lead to high-profile online and social media feedback. And no one wants to be the subject of a bad review. Again this isn't possible without some form of checklist process to follow to ensure it all gets done.

But again, delighting customers requires that employees feel empowered to make a difference; to spot and seize opportunities to go the extra mile, add personal touches, and do whatever it takes to impress. It also relies on these flourishes of inspiration not being inhibited by process.

Inspiring lateral thinking

In his book *The Art of Action*[14], business strategist Stephen Bungay assesses the battle tactics of the Prussian army, to illustrate how to close the gap between plans, actions and results. Rather than plan for every eventuality, and issue commands from the top, Prussian army leaders would set a mission objective and give as short an instruction as possible.

---

[14] The Art of Action - How Leaders Close the Gaps Between Plans, Actions and Results, Stephen Bungay, 2010: http://www.stephenbungay.com/Books.ink.

The idea being that individuals in the battlefield would have the freedom to determine how they would achieve their objectives, and think through for themselves how to overcome whatever barriers they came across.

This new way of behaving was a difficult adjustment at first, as troops had been punished previously for not following orders. So the Army faced a huge amount of work to reverse the existing psychology, rewarding people when they used their initiative - even if things went wrong. Crucially, commanders rewarded the use of initiative, rather than actual outcomes.

This is the approach we advocate, to drive the kind of thinking and behaviour we want to see - which is proactive rather than passive. It involves people determining for themselves the best course of action as new circumstances present themselves and then, as they determine what works and what doesn't, building appropriate parameters and guidance into the evolving process – effectively sharing and fostering best practice.

If your organisation doesn't have any documented processes currently, there is an opportunity for team members to help define and shape those earliest formal process foundations as they are set down. Rather than wait until a later stage to get employees' input and ideas for process improvement, why not let them help determine the way things are done from day one? They know what they're doing, they've learnt as they go, and they're probably already operating in a certain way that has repeatedly proven effective. If they are the ones to document the process, imagine how much more readily they will spot scope for new efficiencies and other improvements.

Another valuable tip, when thinking about documenting and capturing a process, is that it is far easier to get people to actually perform the activity, and note it down as they do it, rather than for them to try to recall every step from memory later, in a meeting room. Once all the steps have been captured, you can save this as your template process.

Remember that, while giving employees the freedom to think and act outside of the process is important, setting down agreed guidelines and making these readily accessible, provides valuable support to new or temporary team members as they feel their way into new situations.

The documented process doesn't need to be perfect. It is far better to have an imperfect process that's changing and improving, than to try to set every detail so deeply in stone that the process is rendered static - and even *dis*empowering, because its comprehensive coverage of 'what to do' feels overwhelming.

12

PROCESS IS ABOUT CHANGE

Change is never easy, and the human race in particular seems slow and reluctant to adapt once it has grown comfortable with a particular way of doing things.

Yet in today's competitive business world, 'agility', 'adaptability' and 'responsiveness' are considered vital qualities. Markets are being disrupted all the time, and consumer preferences can seem to change with the wind - which means that businesses can have a hard time keeping up unless they are attuned to evolving trends and able to regroup around them. In other words, the importance of being able to continuously adapt and move forward should not be underestimated.

When you run a business, there are likely to be many occasions when you will have to agree with your employees to change the way that something is done. But actually making that change happen is another matter.

At cShare, before my leadership/process epiphany, this used to frustrate me greatly. We would agree to change something and I would set reminders in my calendar to check whether whatever we'd agreed had been done in, say, three months' time. In one instance, we agreed we would contact all clients a month before any new software release, to build awareness and encourage them to take advantage of any new features. Yet, when I checked again in a couple of months' time, nothing was happening.

Often, people didn't remember what they had agreed to do, and there was an overall lack of accountability for implementing these kinds of activity. The upshot of all this was that I struggled to trust people to take the baton and run with it once changes had been discussed and agreed. As a result, I would take more of this onto my own shoulders. Sadder still, I would record how often agreed changes were being followed through or not. The findings were quite alarming: agreed changes were only being actioned 60 percent of the time.

I had two choices. I could either switch up the control and be more heavy-handed (hardly likely to have a positive outcome), or try to determine when and why some changes were not being adopted.

As it turned out, it came down to whether employees appreciated the need for a change, and saw the value in the new agreed measures. If the need for change was obvious, staff more typically bought into it. If they were less convinced, inertia tended to win. Another realisation was the importance of being able to see quick results, once changes were made. If staff could see why we had done something, and what the tangible benefits were, this helped hugely with acceptance and buy-in. Which in turn made it easier to implement other changes as these were needed.

Most people mistakenly think process is about maintaining the status quo, locking down how a business operates and keeping this consistent. Actually, I see process as a mechanism for facilitating and implementing *change*.

In the latter days of my old business, eShare, I began to observe that at management meetings over half of the actions we agreed involved process change. If an issue was traced back to an employee not understanding something, we would improve our employee on-boarding procedure. If an error occurred for a client, we could follow this back to the way we deployed our software and introduce extra checks to the way we did this.

If something had gone awry when following up client payments, and we could tie that back to the way that we added invoice information in our system, we would change our debt-collection procedure. If a problem emerged with the functionality or performance of a product, we were able to go back and refine our testing procedure.

Everything that we were doing as a business, all the progress we were making, was being improved by embedding it in process. Process was being used as an effective tool for change - which is not how most people perceive process.

We learnt for ourselves, as a company, that running a fantastic business relies on processes being improved all the time, in every aspect.

13

PROCESS IS EVERYWHERE

When I talk about process, I don't only mean the top 10 core processes in your business. Indeed, many businesses have an automated mechanism or detailed software for managing core processes. I'm referring to the myriad of other processes involved in running your business day to day, that you want to see handled a certain way to ensure consistency, quality and so on.

We've already discussed processes for employee on-boarding, customer on-boarding, lead generation and finances. But process rigour and improvements could also be extended to tasks including:

- Weekly sales reviews;
- The way meetings are run;
- Decisions about suppliers;
- Assessing/reviewing recruitment agencies or other external partners;
- Employment decisions;
- Handling telephone calls and other forms of communication; and so on.

There are also lots of individual processes, where people carry out routine activities over and over again. For example, your sales people will do pitches; your finance people will call clients to collect debts; and your operations people will produce and refine your product. Breaking down each of these repeatable tasks into steps can be illuminating, can be used as the basis for setting down guidelines for new people coming into the given role, and can form the basis for process review and refinement.

When a company wakes up to the importance of process, it makes sense to start with core, cross-department processes that are essential to the success of our business. But actually, all the other processes that contribute to the running and smooth operation of that business are just as important. So, embracing the culture of the checklist as a supportive and helpful tool across all facets of the organisation will join everything up and provide a more consistent experience and quality of operation at every touch point, both for employees and for anyone engaging with the business from the outside.

Technology makes all of this very easy. The ability to *schedule* a checklist, for instance, is very powerful. As well as prompting people to do something, it can remind them *how* to do something which can be useful if a particular task is complex, new to an individual, or doesn't come around very often.

As an example, I have a personal payment that I have to make every month, but it isn't straightforward as it's in a foreign currency and involves an Italian bank account. I can never remember how to operate the bank account, and I don't speak Italian so I don't know which buttons to press. So I set up a monthly process to follow, and documented what I needed to do. This reminds me exactly how to operate my bank account each time this payment is due, so that I don't have to go through the same rigmarole each time, of trying to figure out what each Italian word means.

By setting down the process, it's much simpler to take care of and I don't need to try to commit the steps to memory.

I also have a process for packing my suitcase when I go on holiday, to make sure I take all my items with me. Previously I would inevitably forget something each time I went away - my toothbrush, deodorant, a belt, a pair of shoes, or my phone charger. Rarely the same item, but always something! It also means I never worry about packing until at most 1 hour before we leave home even if we are going away for a month.

By writing a standard trip checklist, and ticking that off each time I go away, I am now assured of never forgetting anything. This removes the stress of packing, and gives me new head-space to think what else I might like to take away with me. So, I now pack a jar of my favourite coffee because I can. Or if it's a night away in a hotel, I might take a bottle of wine and a corkscrew. I even schedule reminders in advance; 2 weeks before I travel to check I have necessary visas and 2 days before I travel to download films for the plane.

Having a process for even the seemingly simple things means that nothing is left to chance, and there is a greater likelihood of everything being done perfectly – consistently, every time. So, by all means concentrate on getting your core business processes documented, but don't underestimate the value of carrying through this rigour into the furthest reaches of your organisation. Your employees will soon start to see the value of process – from the most important things to the tiny little things – because of its indispensable role in ensuring that everything they do is completed in the best way possible, every time.

14

PROCESS IS FUN (Really!)

Okay, bear with me here. I genuinely believe that process is fun and that, with the right application, it can lead to a state of bliss (I was not being ironic when I chose the name of my new business, Process Bliss.). I may be slightly unusual in my thinking, but let me explain.

Process is a way to make things stick, especially the little things that can sometimes make the biggest difference. I doubt I would manage to remember to take coffee every time I go on holiday, without process. I might more readily remember my toothbrush but, without a checklist to guide me, I am less likely to routinely recall the finishing touches that I know will enhance my travel experience. Process helps me to close that gap, taking care of the little things as well as the basics - and without creating extra work for myself as I try to remember everything from scratch each time I go away.

I believe this is the potential of process in a business, and where things become more interesting and, dare I say it, exciting. Not just in streamlining core activity, but in capturing and making it easy for people to see to the subtler details, the brand differentiators - an organisation's added value.

If I go back to recruitment, and specifically the approach I decided I wanted us to take at Process Bliss (selecting people based on talent first, rather than experience), I had to think through with my team what steps would need to be involved to get to this outcome. Because the approach I wanted to take was at odds with traditional ways of identifying and assessing candidates, I felt we needed some structure so that we didn't fall back into old patterns.

My rationale for focusing on talent first, as discussed earlier in the book, was that this can't be taught – whereas experience can be gained. So, I wanted to devise a mechanism for assessing talent. I also wanted to de-emphasise candidates' CVs, because typically these are heavily geared to people's experience.

That's not to say we didn't rate, or want, people's experience. It's just that I wanted to focus on the particular experience we needed candidates to have; I also wanted to find a way to see and test candidates' talent as part of the interview process. So I did some research into aptitude tests, and came up with something we would use in certain circumstances which we captured as part of our process.

I also wanted to have some fun with the interview process and do some things differently. I liked the idea of an interview day, where candidates would work with each other to see how they operated as a group. And the prospect of then taking them out of the office and outside of a work scenario – perhaps going for a walk or for a coffee, to create a different kind of interview tone and setting.

The goal was to do everything we could to make ourselves attractive as an employer, which meant presenting ourselves differently. The aptitude tests we came up with were game-based and fun. We also sent out a gift when candidates were accepted for interviews, to make them feel special. We hadn't figured out the details completely, but I felt confident in what we were doing because everything was part of an evolving process. The process became a facilitator for experimentation and innovation.

Usually, business owners/managers will think up these great ideas as they're going along. Ultimately, they know they might be able to implement them once, during the immediate recruitment task, but they're not really setting down a template to help ensure the new ideas become built into business-as-usual.

In our case, I knew the next tranche of recruitment was not going to be done by me. One of my team would be doing the hiring, so I needed a mechanism to make sure that they did all the things I had planned. At the same time, I didn't want to impose this authoritatively from above: I needed to allow for others to add their own input – not least because I thought there was a lot more that could be done to make our recruitment process even more fun and special.

By putting a process in place, and a documented checklist to follow, I had created a way of making my ideas stick so that they became part of routine activity. This enabled me to start implementing initiatives that in other businesses would struggle to get off the ground, or peter out over time – just because busy people instinctively revert to the way things have always been done, the path of least resistance.

I'm not saying we're unique in our ambitions. I've seen other businesses welcome new staff with a welcome cake or box of chocolates on their desk on their first day, or by sending out a relevant book when the chosen candidate accepts a job offer. We chose to send out a Process Bliss T-shirt to make new-joiners feel they are now one of the team.

We take a similar approach when we secure a new client. As we sign them up we send out a gift, along with a relevant interesting fact. At my former business, eShare, we used to send an unusual wooden gift with an interesting fact about the place in Moldova where it was made. Did you know Moldova was home to the world's largest biscuit? Clients loved it.

It never hurts to get a relationship off on a strong footing, creating a positive and memorable first impression. Surprising and delighting someone from day one helps set the right tone and makes a business stand out from the crowd.

Process application: when to leave well enough alone

In essence, process applies everywhere. But not every aspect of day-to-day business needs a formal checklist and the support of workflow-based software (the proposition of my business, Process Bliss) for it to work.

Processes that are very fluid or easy to remember are probably best left alone, especially if they're already happening without issue. So, for example, the process for opening our office in the morning probably doesn't need to be formalised, tweaked or documented. But in a kitchen retail store environment, the desired experience may be more involved, thus benefiting from some process magic. Steps might include ensuring the answerphone is off; making the premises smell inviting by baking some bread; or erecting signs outside the shop to catch the eye of passers-by.

The more convoluted the process, and the greater the chance of someone missing a step, the more valuable some process support will be. So the key question to ask is, to what extent are you confident that all relevant staff will recall and execute a process, without any prompting? Another consideration is, do you and/or other managers need confirmation that a process is being followed? Will it suffice to simply train people and hope that they will comply with what's required, or do you need a feedback mechanism to track what's going on?

Even if you don't require a feedback mechanism, and you can rely on people to remember what needs to be done, there is still a process: it's just stored in people's heads. And that's fine, until the process becomes more intricate, increasing the risk that important steps may be missed without anyone having insight into why that might be, and any opportunities for improvement that are being lost.

15

"NOSE IN, FINGERS OUT"

We've talked about the mechanisms for implementing process, and also how to do it. But there is another major change needed as part of the broader transition. I call this "nose in, 'fingers out" - with reference specifically to owner/managers or other senior executives. This is about senior figures letting go of the reins, and learning not to meddle as teams take ownership of their own processes. They should still retain a close interest in how the business is doing (nose in), but without interfering in the day-to-day detail (fingers out).

It is a fine balance, and can take some getting used to. After years of micro-managing everything, it would be very easy for leaders to decamp to a beach in another time zone, leaving the business to run itself. But this could lead to anarchy, or a sense that the senior management have mentally disengaged and left their employees to do all the work while they toy with semi-retirement.

Finding the right balance is about recognising that the business is a set of processes which needs to be enabled, shaped, overseen and kept on course by the business leadership.

Positively communicating the changes, and the motivation behind them, and easing the transition to the new normal/more structured way of working will be critical. Employees may feel unsettled by what's being entrusted to them, and leaders are likely to feel nervous about relinquishing control.

Not all employees will feel comfortable with the new set-up, as part of which they are being encouraged to manage their own work and show initiative. Some may prefer just turning up to work, being told what to do, taking their salary and going home again. And, through a process of self-selection, they may gradually move on to one of the many businesses that still fosters that way of behaving.

By contrast, there will be many more people who will thrive in the rebooted business environment, who rise to the challenge and embrace the autonomy. But even these employees will take time to adjust. In the meantime, managers may need to sit on their hands and see how the situation unfolds, remaining on hand to offer support, but refraining from issuing directions.

With the right encouragement and gentle nurturing, behaviour will begin to change. As long as managers can resist the temptation to interfere, green shoots should start to appear before long. In the meantime, business leaders can focus on looking inward, on changes they too can start to make, to show employees that things are different. This may involve changes to the way they talk to staff, to tease out feedback and input – by asking questions, probing more deeply and discussing employees' ideas, rather than shooting them down where this might once have been the first instinct.

I'll admit, this can be a difficult adjustment for business leaders used to being at the centre of everything with their sleeves rolled up - never rating anyone else's suggestions, or commitment to the cause, above their own. I certainly found it hard at first to release control and trust more.

The key is to understand that you still have a say in and indeed the power of veto over everything that happens. You don't have to agree to anything silly being implemented; you just need to listen and see what is suggested. And when you *are* slower to dismiss ideas, you will often find that there is always something of value in them. Once you allow other people's proposals to be aired and discussed, resulting in a brainstorm, there is every chance you'll arrive at a far better solution than you could have possibly thought of yourself.

"Once you allow other people's proposals to be aired and discussed, resulting in a brainstorm, there is every chance you'll arrive at a far better solution than you could have possibly thought of yourself."

Redefining the CEO's remit

As, slowly but surely, leaders learn to let go of control over day-to-day processes, they will soon find they have time for the higher-level strategic duties they are supposed to be responsible for.

I am a member of a business mastermind group of about 12 CEOs: we meet regularly and discuss our businesses in detail. I thoroughly recommend this: it is one of the things that has helped me to transform my business and release myself from working crazy hours. It provides me with a chance to step back from the business one day a month, and to learn and develop my own skills. It's surprising how transformative this can be - both in a work context and from a personal perspective.

Early on in these meetings we explored 'What's the role of a CEO?'. It was fascinating that most of the 12 CEOs in the room, despite being in their jobs for a fair amount of time, had not had any CEO training. As with many SME business leaders, most had come into the role after having a great idea, inheriting a business, being promoted or becoming involved in a spin-off of a company, without really understanding much about what's involved.

After some consideration, and in pairs, we listed the various aspects to the role of a CEO as we saw them, which someone then collated on a board at the front. The tasks were many and varied: sales; attracting clients; overseeing operations; getting funding; managing finances; managing the team; and so much more.

This wasn't supposed to be a list of overarching high-level responsibilities; it was more about what we actually do and get involved in on a daily basis. So effectively we were all saying, 'We do sales, we do marketing, we do product development, we do operations, we do customer service, we do relationships...' By the time we had finished, there must have been more than 20 categories of activity listed.

At this point, I felt disheartened, thinking, "Well, this can't be right. We can't be doing *everything*. Is this right? The job of a CEO is actually doing everything?"

Ironically, it was those things that *hadn't* been written on the board that I now know to be the remit of a CEO, namely:

- Responsibility for setting the vision of the business;
- Building the culture;
- The six leadership styles;
- Building the team;
- Structuring the business so that it runs itself;
- Ensuring the CEO's vision is communicated to all employees; and
- Ensuring everybody is doing their jobs and performing to high standards.

It was a valuable exercise in reflection. Most of the CEOs in the room were working *in* their business rather than working *on* their business. They all saw their remit as that of an overarching being, who looked after this entity that was supposed to be succeeding. They saw it as their responsibility to identify where something was not performing, or where someone wasn't doing a great job, and then delve in and fix the problem or fill the resulting gap.

But actually, these are not the responsibilities of a CEO. Rather, it is up to you to structure your business so that employees have the tools they need to perform, and so that the people you hire are the best suited to the work.

It is your job to facilitate all of this, not to clean up the mess when poor practice plays out to its logical conclusion. There's no point expending effort furiously trying to bail out a leaky boat below deck if it's sailing straight towards an iceberg. Someone needs to be keeping a lookout and making sure the business is on the right course. But of the 12 CEOs in that room, I felt many, including me, were so busy trying to plug holes that they could no longer see the horizon.

Over my years with this group, I've watched all of those CEOs evolve and grow – myself included. It was at my very first meeting that I picked up the phrase, "Nose in, fingers out", which to this day remains a succinct reminder to me to stay at the helm and not meddle below deck.

There is another very good reason why CEOs should know and keep to their place, and that's in the interests of staff morale. If the top person in the company keeps feeling the need to wade in and sort things out, what does this say about their trust in their staff? Yes, there may be issues to be sorted out, but again the CEO should play the role of facilitator – inviting employees to share in a discussion about what has gone wrong, and what might be done to put things right – rather than as someone who swoops in to unpick the mess that staff have created.

A defined process, with a built-in feedback mechanism, can help keep everyone from overstepping their boundaries, placing blame, or spiralling into negativity. If the process-supporting software has captured any issues in real time, already there is a neutral place to start any investigations into what has gone awry, and to form the basis of a discussion around potential solutions.

Again, this all comes back to the importance of process as a tool that drives success – for individuals, for teams, for the business, and for the CEO who can now spend more time looking to the future and where to steer the ship next.

If we drill down into a CEO's role in more detail, we soon realise that it is all about process. Our job as business leaders is to enable process and make it work smoothly, which in turn involves:

- Enabling teams to communicate;
- Making sure staff have the tools they need to get things right;
- Providing and facilitating a way to find out where help and supporting information exists;
- Encouraging employees to come up with new ideas;
- Applying direction and a filter to how new ideas are considered and debated;
- Implementing new ideas in the business; and
- Finding a way to make any changes and improvements stick.

These are the types of challenges that should command your attention as CEO. And it was to liberate business leaders from the distractions of day-to-day problem-solving and general meddling that I came up with the idea for Process Bliss.

I built the software originally as a tool to help me to control my business: to automate this frustrating job that I was doing. At that point, my intention was to be able to dictate to my staff how they should do things, in quite an authoritarian way: "This is the process you must follow, and this is how it has to be followed – oh, and I'm going to be tracking it to see that everyone has conformed."

Looking back, I am not surprised that my team essentially revolted, rejecting the software and the process it set out because I had sought to stymie their creativity and remove their freedom, and in so doing kill any enthusiasm or motivation to do their jobs well. Another reason it failed miserably was because, when you get to a sizeable business of about 40 to 50 people, there is no way that one individual can write prescriptive mechanisms to underpin every aspect of what people do. Rather, the 50 people in the business need to have a say in how those processes evolve, based on their first-hand understanding of what works and what doesn't, and their respective insight into what might help alleviate any issues.

When it finally dawned that I was being too controlling, triggering nothing but stress and unhappiness on all sides, I took a step back and said, "Actually, just ignore me – what do ***you*** think needs to happen?"

Once I reversed the paradigm, and saw that what I actually needed to do was give my staff a tool that would help them, not me, our world tilted on its axis – and suddenly the outlook grew brighter. Staff embraced the software tools as their own, as something that would support them to do a better job.

For my part, despite having the means to check in and watch over what was unfolding, I found that I did not do this. I had let go. The mechanics were in place to drive best practice, and for staff to hone this. I felt reassured and liberated. And as a result staff started to feel trusted.

We all felt a lot freer, and much - ***much*** - happier.

16

GETTING STARTED

I've implemented many new initiatives in my businesses over the years, and learnt a lot in the process. It's quite fascinating when consultants come in and suggest new ideas. I find sales consultants are probably the worst. They come in and they present a methodology, which is fantastic and clever, and really well thought through. They charge you for the report and recommendations and then they hand it over and say, "This is what you need to do." They act as though 90 percent of the work has been done and now there's just the simple matter of the remaining 10 percent – the implementation - to complete the transformation. As though this were the simple part!

Almost invariably, consultants seem to operate on this basis – yet it's in the implementation phase that businesses really struggle. The easy bit is spouting some theory and maybe tweaking it to fit a business. The hardest part is actually applying this theory in a real business when there may be 50, 500 or even 5000, people affected by the change – people who will need to be taken on the journey, and supported through the transition, to minimise resistance and maximise buy-in and ownership of the 'new normal'.

A sales consultant once advised me that it was really important to map out the customer journey – in other words mapping our sales process to our customer's buying process at every stage. We spent £18,000 on a lot of consulting work with this individual. But when we received the report at the end of the day, with the sales process set out and these activities we were supposed to do, we had no idea how to make this take effect in the business. We all looked at it and loved the theory, but nothing much really changed even though I tried hard to implement the new proposed behaviour within our systems.

At that point the consultant walked away with her fee, leaving me with the report. I'm a reasonably intelligent person, but I simply could not work out how to make the change happen in my business – the consultant provided me with no support to help me deliver against her plan and when I asked for that help and guidance she had nothing to offer.

So I am keen to make sure I don't leave you in the same predicament – armed with a vision of how great practical, software-supported process can be – but without a mechanism to change the way your business is run. As far as I'm concerned, I've really only done 10 percent of the work in setting out a vision for change – applying and implementing this within your business is all still to do, and I am more pragmatic than the sales consultant I encountered: because I acknowledge that this is actually 90 percent of the transformation.

The good news is that I don't think the implementation I am proposing is very difficult – ***and*** I plan to guide you through the next steps.

1. **Identify between one and three processes to tackle**

Pick on between one and three processes that are really causing you to suffer. These are likely to have the following characteristics:

- They are important to your business.
- They frustrate you because they could be so much better.
- They are complicated with lots of steps.
- They involve multiple people and departments working together.

I say between one and three because it is really important to get some results quickly and if you start to deal with too many processes at once you will lose interest and get bogged down before you and your team see any benefits.

Almost always people start by trying to document every single process in the business. One client of mine produced 231 processes. Please, please don't do this. We can build other processes later. Ideally just start with up to three, preferably that all relate to one area of business e.g. finance, HR, or customer service.

2. **<u>Capture how things work</u>**

The next thing you need to do is to capture how things work right now – preferably by noting this down as it happens. At this point people get hung up on getting every minute detail written down however I'd rather you didn't spend too long. In fact I insist you do this quite superficially. The second biggest mistake you can make is getting bogged down on this. It doesn't matter about the detail because we are going to refine this process over time. We just need a starting point.

And the biggest mistake people make - they start to redesign everything. Please do not start redesigning anything. Just capture it as it is right now.

If you start redesigning, you will again get bogged down and it doesn't matter because this process will be improved and refined later.

The reason people want to redesign at this stage is they have the mindset that we are going to lock down these processes. But remember, the opposite is true, we are going to release them to wonderfully evolve.

3. <u>Make it collaborative</u>

Obviously, we've developed software to help you do this at Process Bliss, but you could just as easily start with a spreadsheet for this stage. I think Google Sheets is great because it's collaborative; or you could use Microsoft Office Online as an alternative.

If you use a spreadsheet then create a tab for each process you have selected. Now get everybody involved to provide their input, writing out what they do and where they fit in. There is no need to represent this as Visio diagrams or as complex workflows. A list is best.

4. <u>Closely define the remit of outsiders</u>

If you get process consultants involved, you will likely find they devote all their time to drawing up these amazing diagrams that are really complex but which, in reality, nobody looks at. Far better to work with something practical – such as a check-list. Simply draw up a column of activities, perhaps with a responsibility for each column if you want, as well as a description, if additional information is needed. See figure 16.1.

Process Name: Employee Onboarding

Step Number	Activity	Step Description	Responsibility	Resources
1	Welcome meeting	Book a meeting and run through with the new employee: - Employee org chart - Health & safety practices - How to book a meeting room - How to request holiday & log absence	Sandra Jones	Link to Employee org chart
2	Review policies	Assign policies for attestation to the new employee and inform HR	Sandra Jones	HR email address: HR@alisteresam.com HR Phone Extension 4087
3	Company values & mission meeting	Line manager or CEO to explain company values and mission statement.	Alister Esam	Company values are stored at: D:\Company Info\Values
4	Add employee to payroll	Obtain P45 and enroll payroll database	Doug Smith	Link to payroll system
5	Add employee to company org chart		Jenny Evans	
etc				

Employee onboarding ▾ Employee Offboarding ▾ Disciplinary ▾ ← Tab for each process

Figure 16.1

If people need to access or prepare a document to perform an activity (such as a contract for sale, an employment contract or a policy guideline), simply create a link to these documents, assuming you have them stored online, by providing a hyperlink in a fifth column. If they aren't stored online just record the file location (see figure 16,2). That's it, you have your first process!

Process Name: Employee Onboarding

Step Number	Activity	Step Description	Responsibility	Resources
1	Welcome meeting	Book a meeting and run through with the new employee: - Employee org chart - Health & safety practices - How to book a meeting room - How to request holiday & log absence	Sandra Jones	Link to Employee org chart
2	Review policies	Assign policies for attestation to the new employee and inform HR	Sandra Jones	HR email address: HR@alisteresam.com HR Phone Extension 4087
3	Company values & mission meeting	Line manager or CEO to explain company values and mission statement	Alister Esam	Company values are stored at D:\Company Info\Values
4	Add employee to payroll	Obtain P45 and enroll payroll database	Doug Smith	Link to payroll system
5	Add employee to company org chart		Jenny Evans	
etc				

Link to a docu

Contact det

Figure 16.2

5. Embed them in your business

Whether you use specific software or spreadsheets, next, what's needed is a means for people to confirm that they've performed the activities required by their part of the process. By doing this you are connecting the documentation to the activities you perform. This is where people who create documents go wrong, no one looks at them and they become out of date.

If you've set out the process in a collaborative space, with people's names against all of the steps in a sequence, it becomes easy for people to see their responsibilities. You could even use a data filter to help them easily identify their own activities. Each time you need to use a process, add a column for that task. So for example if you have an employee onboarding process documented in the sheet then each time you onboard an employee, add a column with the name of the employee. See figure 16.3.

Process Name: Employee Onboarding

Name of employee

Step Number	Activity	Step Description	Rav Patel	April Small	Ken Simpson
1	Welcome meeting	Book a meeting and run through with the new employee: - Employee org chart - Health & safety practices - How to book a meeting room - How to request holiday & log absence	13/05	13/05	19/05
2	Review policies	Assign policies for attestation to the new employee and inform HR	27/06	17/05	25/07
3	Company values & mission meeting	Line manager or CEO to explain company values and mission statement.		15/05	
4	Add employee to payroll	Obtain P45 and enroll payroll database		18/05	
5	Add employee to company org chart		19/7	21/5	
etc					

Date of activity performed

Figure 16.3

This column can then be used to register when someone has completed each element in the process. While a tick would suffice, I prefer employees to record the date they completed the step, because that's a more useful piece of information that will allow you to analyse the process later – as part of a review of what works well or not so well, and as the basis for future improvements.

Collaborating on a simple document which sets everything out clearly is the most important thing here, to keep things straightforward and get everyone involved. I wouldn't worry about trying to control the spreadsheet or adding permissions to it. Just trust your staff to be able to put something together. If you want controls over the process, that's where software can start to play a part.

6. Introduce a feedback loop

We need to capture feedback so we can improve. For each time you run the process now add another column for feedback that allows people to comment on each of the current steps and provide constructive feedback. See figure 16.4.

Process Name: Employee Onboarding

Step Number	Activity	Step Description	Rav Patel	Feedback	April Small	Feedback
1	Welcome meeting	Book a meeting and run through with the new employee - Employee org chart - Health & safety practices - How to book a meeting room - How to request holiday & log absence	13/05	I think we should also cover office security	13/05	I think a link to the HR policies would be helpful here
2	Review policies	Assign policies for attestation to the new employee and inform HR	27/06		17/05	
3	Company values & mission meeting	Line manager or CEO to explain company values and mission statement			15/05	
4	Add employee to payroll	Obtain P45 and enroll payroll database			18/05	
5	Add employee to company org chart		19/7		21/5	I think we should do this step before they join - would look much better
etc						

Suggested improvements

Figure 16.4

Nothing needs to be set in stone here. When you review the spreadsheet, you might consider whether additional elements need to be added, or certain steps honed. Locking down the spreadsheet as a definitive record of process suggests finality and rigidity – rather than promoting a culture of continuous improvement and process innovation.

I would go one step further and suggest that, if someone wants to add a new step to improve the process, the facility is there to allow this – then the team can see how this new measure pans out in practice, and how useful it is to everyone involved.

7. Keep an audit trail

I recommend keeping an audit trail, which could be a simple case of making a copy of the spreadsheet periodically, so that you can see where steps or details are added or deleted, and/or gain insights into where parts of the process might not be as effective as originally thought.

8. Once it's working, extend it

Only once you have buy into the approach and it is delivering value should you extend it. But then it is a matter of identifying further processes and departments and gradually rolling the approach out where it makes most sense. If you decide to extend this approach to more processes in the business then having that all within one spreadsheet can be too complex. A better approach is often to create a spreadsheet per department. This allows you then to manage permissions on each spreadsheet appropriately. That said there is no reason why members of one department can't have access to another department's spreadsheet if they need to see progress or if they play a role in those processes.

9. Consider software

Obviously this is now getting more complex and it is at this point at which you may want to consider using some checklist software such as Process Bliss to manage this. That is basically how Process Bliss was born. I initially did use spreadsheets but found I needed to develop Process Bliss to give me the extra permission, reporting, audit trail, todo list, feedback, rich documentation, integration with other systems and wealth of other features that I needed. I'll cover this more later.

10. Accelerate improvement that sticks

At eShare, we used to have weekly senior leadership team meetings, as part of which we would spend an hour resolving challenges within the business. Each week, we'd typically get through four or five issues.

The most powerful aspect of those meetings was the process changes. During one session, for example, we discussed an issue with a customer who was unhappy. Their software deployment hadn't gone very well, it turned out, because they wanted their historical data to be loaded onto the system before it was shared with users (who happened to be senior board members) and our team had not scoped or included this as part of the project.

Having reviewed the situation, we agreed that in future – as part of the initial fact-finding exercise when we took on a customer – we would ask them about any requirements concerning historical data.

By offering that service as an additional chargeable piece of work for the client if they wanted it doing, this would add value for the client and create additional revenue for us. The key point from a process perspective, though, was that we agreed to build this into the client scoping process, so that this would be offered as standard for every customer going forward. The problem was fixed once and for all and forever.

We took the action straight from the meeting and implemented it into our existing process. That's not rocket science but what was so important about having a process was from then on, we knew that step would be carried out ad infinitum, or at least until we made a proactive decision to stop doing it or to change it.

Before we implemented the software now known as Process Bliss, only about 60 percent of the changes we agreed at senior leadership team meetings were still in effect six months later. But by being able to incorporate the current action within a living, breathing, documented process, the new step could not be ignored or scrapped without a deliberate decision to remove it from the spreadsheet. If that did not happen - because the new step had positive results - the change stuck until a proactive decision otherwise

It's important not to create too many barriers that might prevent employees from improving process. But if you do decide to go further than a spreadsheet and implement process-checklist software, you will gain useful controls around who is permitted to add or remove steps to/from a templated process. It is far better to give staff the ability to constructively change and evolve a process than it is to risk curbing their creativity, though, so consider any controls carefully before potentially complicating matters.

In conclusion, whether you approach process consistency via a spreadsheet or via checklist software or indeed using paper checklists, what's important is to provide the tools for everyone to see what needs to be done and a requirement to log activities as being completed. Linking in additional guidance, shortcuts to relevant resources and the latest information will turn these tools into something indispensable, that employees want to use because it makes their job easier and removes the stress of trying to remember the subtler nuances of how to complete tasks well.

The most important action really is just to get started.

The gap between theory & practical application

Of course, there are a great many revelations that are powerful in theory, but when you come to applying them in the real world, their potential doesn't always transfer.

A simple analogy is telling an overweight person they need to eat less. It's fairly obvious to me that if I want to become more svelte in appearance, I should eat less and exercise more. The difficulty is not educating me about the calories in the food, or that fish and chips are bad for me, or that drinking too much alcohol is going to tip the scales, or that exercise is going to make me healthier – everybody knows that. But knowing isn't the same as doing. The difficult part is actually how you motivate someone – yourself, even - to get out of bed every morning at 7am and go for a run. And to do this routinely, not just for the first few days of January after renewing the annual pledge to get fit.

Business process is not all that different. Team members might say, "Oh, we should be doing the customer on-boarding in a different way." So, they go and try something new for the next three customers, before inertia wins and they revert to old habits.

If you're going to implement new ambitions and make lasting changes, you need a methodology to embed that change - something beyond good intentions.

Why use process software?

At a time where we've got so much technology and everyone has access to computers and the Internet, why not just use spreadsheets in your business? You might be thinking, "Yeah, process is great. I'm going to set up my own spreadsheet."

Spreadsheets are pretty good, and certainly better than nothing for instilling a bit more rigour around how things are done. But process software also offers a means of control over how process is implemented.

If you have a spreadsheet everyone can edit, add to or reduce, there's nothing really to stop someone simply wiping your process altogether. You can keep a backup of it, of course, but if an important step is inadvertently or deliberately deleted, you might not notice for months, and the consequences could be profound.

One of the advantages of our Process Bliss software is that it allows people to feed into the template process, but the leader retains the right to approve or veto any proposed changes. You can still encourage feedback, and collate this easily, but it's up to you to determine what happens next.

The three options are:

- You will ignore it.
- You will make the change suggested; or
- You will do something differently.

The key is having some structure around ongoing process innovation and transformation, and strong process software will facilitate that.

The additional advantage of a purpose-built software solution is the added scope for collaboration and rules-driven workflow. With a spreadsheet alone, there is nothing to prompt people to actually perform any activity, whereas with purpose-developed software like Process Bliss you can set up alerts and notifications to be sent to designated people, either to prompt them that their activity is now due, or that a problem has arisen with a previous step, for example. So, rather than a process stalling, targeted action can be taken in a timely fashion.

There are other, subtler controls available too. For instance, you can set permissions so that certain people don't see certain processes.

There's also the potential to integrate the process software with other systems – so that your accounting system triggers a payment chasing process when an invoice settlement is overdue, for example. Or, when you recruit a new employee, this activity could automatically generate a record in the company's HR system.

With a spreadsheet, the scope for analysing, tightening and transforming process will be quite basic. With Process Bliss, by contrast, there is the potential for powerful insight and reporting into whether and how tasks are being performed, where any issues are arising, allowing additional rules to be put in place. A straightforward tick-box can't systematically provide for those tweaks; there is nothing to stop people skipping steps or 'lying' to say something was done when actually the opposite was true. Process software like ours builds in scope for exceptions management – that is, for staff to log when a step wasn't possible, or was bypassed, and why – providing a useful audit trail along with constructive feedback from those involved, recorded in real time, creating valuable information for those in charge.

17

CONCLUSION

My journey to building Process Bliss began with my own experience, as an accidental CEO of a business without any real training to be in that role. My assumption that I needed to be in control of everything made for a stressful time for everyone. For me personally, it was a miserable time - and over the years I have found it astonishing how many other CEOs say that their business is making them equally unhappy.

When a business is making its founder/owner/manager stressed and distraught, it's usually because process isn't functioning properly. If you're in that position right now, I hope that the lessons I've learnt can help you.

By developing and applying Process Bliss at eShare, I was able to transform both my old company and my life, reducing my time on the job to a *fifth* of what it had been! While not quite making myself redundant, I was able to let go and extract myself from the day-to-day detail, and my controlling obsession with checking that everyone was doing their jobs as I expected.

This paradigm shift meant that the business effectively ran itself, and I was eventually able to sell eShare and walk away. The key was not all the extra hours I had put in, but rather the proper structure I had put in place and the fact that I'd equipped my staff with the tools they needed to confidently do their jobs well and consistently. This might sound like an amazing feat, but actually the biggest barrier to progress had been me!

"While not quite making myself redundant, I was able to let go and extract myself from the day-to-day detail, and my controlling obsession with checking that everyone was doing what I expected."

So, you may need to expect some initial discomfort when you first start to loosen the reins on your business, and trust your staff to run things themselves. When you first let go and relinquish control, it can be a little disconcerting. But it is all worth it when you realise how it will transform your life, making your business more successful and more independent from you. So, I would urge you to make the leap.

While of course I would say that Process Bliss is the ideal solution, I'm not actually suggesting that you implement software in order to be able to bring your processes under control. Transformation starts with thinking differently about your role and about whether staff currently have all the tools they need to perform their roles to the best of their ability.

Here are three things I recommend you do to kick-start your own transformation and recover your work-life balance:

- Accept that it's okay to release control of your business and let other people get involved and run it;

- Give your staff tools to help them, so that they are able to run complex collaborative processes confidently and competently, without having to remember everything; and
- Remove yourself from any gaps you've been trying to bridge and trust your staff to fill them.

Remember: if you're always there to catch a child who looks about to fall off their bike, the child will never learn to ride solo. It's important to take a step back, even if you have to watch them wobble at first. It's by faltering and recovering that we learn. Even if you're worried about the business leaking money during the initial transition, consider this as an essential investment if you are ever to let go.

Final ruminations

As final thoughts, I will first leave you with this quote by Peter Michael Senge, an American systems scientist, senior lecturer at the MIT Sloan School of Management in the US and the founder of the Society for Organizational Learning.

Writing in *The Fifth Discipline: The Art & Practice of The Learning Organization*[15], he notes, "Vision without 'systems thinking' ends up painting lovely pictures of the future, with no deep understanding of the forces that must be mastered to move from here to there."

---

[15] The Fifth Discipline: The Art & Practice of The Learning Organization, Peter M. Senge, 2006 revised edition: https://www.penguinrandomhouse.com/books/163984/the-fifth-discipline-by-peter-m-senge/.

Process delivers that 'systems thinking', making it possible to deliver future vision - without demanding anything unreasonable or impossible from those involved.

On the topic of bliss, meanwhile, consider these wise words from 19th-century French author Alexandre Dumas: "There is neither happiness nor unhappiness in this world; there is only the comparison of one state with another. Only a man who has felt ultimate despair is capable of feeling ultimatc bliss."

And from one business owner who has felt ultimate despair at the helm of a company without good process, I can vouch for the transformation in quality of life, both personally and for those around me, that comes from achieving process enabled serenity. Wherever you are on your process journey, I wish you the same outcome.

Printed in Great Britain

By Book Printing UK